Stand Up and Fight

Overcoming Spiritual
Attacks in your
Personal Life

Stand Up and Fight

Barry Austin
With
Margaret Hudson

Sovereign World

Sovereign World Ltd.
P.O. Box 17
Chichester
England

Unless otherwise stated, quotations are from the New International Version of the Bible. Published by Hodder & Stoughton.

Quotations marked NKJV are taken from the New King James Bible Copyright © Thomas Nelson Publishers Inc. Nashville U.S.A.

Quotations marked RSV are taken from the Revised Standard Version Copyright © Churches of Christ in the United States of America.

The Amplified Bible Copyright © Zondervan Bible Publishers, Grand Rapids, Michigan

British Library Cataloguing in Publication Data
Austin, Barry
  Stand up and fight
  1. Christian life. Self-realisation
  I. Title II. Hudson, Margaret
  248.4

Typeset in Plantin by The Ikthos Studios, Andover, Hampshire. Printed by Clays Ltd, St Ives plc.

Contents

SECTION THREE: "LET'S FIGHT"

SECTION FOUR:
"LET'S FIGHT, TOGETHER"

Foreword

I have known Barry Austin for almost 15 years. During that time I have watched him pastor and disciple hundreds and hundreds of Christian workers and leaders. Everyone who is influenced by Barry comes away a changed person. They are impacted by his godliness, and benefitted by his wisdom and years of experience.

One of the things that attracts people to Barry is his balance. He is not a man who swings from one extreme to another, but he digs into God's Word and comes up with what the Lord says, pulling together different aspects of a truth.

Barry has taken a controversial and sometimes difficult subject, making it practical and down to earth in this book. I believe we often assume that Christians know much more than they do about spiritual warfare. It is extremely important that we have solid teaching on who Satan is, how he attacks Christians, and how God has provided for us to overcome the enemy. Barry does this for us in this book.

It alarms me to see how many Christians in the world are attacked by the spiritual forces of darkness unleashed when Satan fell from heaven, and have no idea that the mental, emotional, relational or physical problems they face have a spiritual dimension to them. When things go wrong there can be many causes, and one of these is that we are being harassed or tempted by Satan or one of his demons. If the Lord Jesus was not above such temptation, dare we think that we will go through life without confronting the spiritual forces of darkness?

I urge every believer to study God's Word carefully, that they might be armed with understanding and authority, in order to combat Satan's minions.

Barry Austin's book assists us to do just that. While focusing on God's character and the victory won for us on the Cross by the Lord Jesus, he forthrightly exposes Satan's schemes and points us to the power and resources that God has made available to us to overcome him.

One of the reasons this book is so helpful is that it is **practical**. It is not just a bunch of theory or mystical theology. Barry gives practical experiences, illustrating how God taught him to discern Satan's attacks and how to overcome them. Every believer who takes time to read this book will be saved many hours of frustration, confusion and spiritual defeat.

I urge every Christian to read this book and I particularly challenge pastors and spiritual leaders to put it in the hands of new Christians. It has been a blessing to me as I trust it will be to you.

Floyd McClung
September 1990

Preface

In some of the stories used in this book, names and unnecessary details have been altered, to protect the identity of the person(s) involved. Alternatively, some incidents described are not actual events which took place but are composites of several incidents. Nevertheless they reflect very real situations.

At the end of each chapter there are a few questions. These are designed not only for individual use but also for group discussion and prayer.

SECTION ONE:
"WE ARE IN A BATTLE"

Chapter 1

The Battle Is On

The sobbing of our ten month baby girl grew louder than ever, her little face reddening every minute. My wife, Kay, had done everything she could – searching to see if a nappy pin was stuck in her, changing the nappy, trying to give her a drink – but all to no avail. Passing the little bundle to me, Kay slumped on the sofa exhausted.

For what seemed like hours I walked up and down the room, attempting to soothe my daughter, but her crying continued. "What on earth is wrong with her? There doesn't seem to be any logical explanation." Inwardly I prayed, "Lord, help us," as I wearily walked yet another length of the living room.

A few moments later a thought quietly interrupted the confusion in my mind: "Take authority over the devil." My instinctive response was, "That's crazy. She's only crying. She's not possessed or anything." Yet as the thought would not be shrugged off, in desperation I concluded, "I've got nothing to lose; I'll give it a try."

Looking at my daughter I said, "In Jesus' name I resist the devil." I was immediately taken aback as the cries instantly ceased and the most beautiful smile enveloped her face as she beamed up at me!

Utterly flabbergasted, I laid my daughter down into her cot and within a few minutes she was sleeping peacefully. Joining Kay on the sofa, I breathed a sigh of relief and then together we asked, "Lord, what was all that about?"

It was Kay who remembered first. Earlier in the day I'd been counselling a young man in our home. He was using drugs and involved in the occult, so he had quite a few problems! I had neglected to ask God for His protection over us as a family before that counselling appointment and as Kay and I talked, we realised that somehow the demonic oppression in this man's life had affected our home – in particular, our daughter.

Many years have gone by since this incident took place and while I hasten to add that I don't believe most crying babies are oppressed by the devil, I am nevertheless convinced that the devil is active in this universe and will try all means to oppose those who want to be involved in building God's kingdom, even to afflicting little babies. Certainly the devil will try to prevent Christians from being effective in their service for the Lord.

Several years ago I worked in an office where I was the only believer. I'd made friends with several of my workmates and I'd managed to talk a little about the Lord with them. The exception was one man about my own age. John and I often went for walks together during the lunchbreak and conversation covered many areas. But whenever I tried to talk about the Lord, we'd either be interrupted or John would be suddenly distracted by something else.

This situation continued for several months, until one evening I began to pray, "Lord why can't I get through to John?" As I kept praying I sensed that there was something spiritual blocking my communication with him and I was also convicted that I'd been trying to witness in my own strength, without really praying for John. So I confessed my independence to the Lord and asked Him to help me.

"Lord, how should I pray for John?" In response to my question, a verse of scripture flashed into my mind. It was one I'd read only a few days earlier, *"The reason the Son of God appeared was to destroy the devil's work"* (1 John 3:8b). As I was reminded of this verse I knew that God was prompting me to resist the devil.

I felt the presence of the Holy Spirit with me as I declared in prayer, "Jesus, the Son of God, appeared to destroy all obstacles in John's life! Lord Jesus, please break through this veil over his mind. And Satan, I resist you in Jesus' name."

A few days later we went for our customary walk. As we talked I mentioned something about the Lord and John became interested. He asked me what had happened to change my life, and I shared the events which had led me to give my life to the Lord. We had a great conversation and I began to marvel at the wonderful answer to prayer.

The devil will try to hinder the efforts of anyone trying to share their faith with others, but we have the authority in Jesus' name to overcome him.

My main reason in writing this book is to encourage us to a greater level of alertness to the influences of the devil in our Christian walk. I believe that often we go through struggles and hindrances in our lives blaming them on circumstances or other people, when in fact many times these difficulties are caused by spiritual forces getting in and interfering, blocking what God wants to do through us.

While we don't want to be looking for the devil

behind every bush, the other extreme is to dismiss his existence altogether, resulting in a passivity amongst many Christians. It's this passivity which I believe God is concerned about and wants us to rise up against; for we are in a battle, and in that battle we need to learn how to stand up and fight.

Jesus clearly states the position. When He first mentions the church, in the same breath He includes the spiritual battle. *"I will build my church,"* Jesus says, *"and the gates of Hades will not overcome it"* (Matthew 16:18).

Why does Jesus talk about the "gates" of Hades? Throughout the Old Testament a number of passages refer to the "elders sitting at the gates" – the elders being the people in authority. The gates therefore represent the place of authority as they either permit or prevent people from passing through them.

Knowing that the disciples will understand that the "gates" represent authority, Jesus then points out to them the location of the gates. They are not the gates of heaven; rather the gates of hell! Therefore the "gates of hell" as used here refers to the authority of Satan.

An alternative translation of the above scripture is, *"the gates of Hades shall not hold out against the church"* (Amplified Bible). So Jesus is not only saying that the authority of Satan will have no holding power over the church, but also that the church is meant to hold power over Satan. We, the church, are to be on the offensive, plundering the strongholds of Satan where people are held captive.[1]

In this book we will look at the nature of these strongholds and how they got there in the first place. But more importantly we will focus on the victory which Jesus has won on the Cross and the provision

He has made for us to live in that victory. Rather than being passive people, we are called to be actively involved with Jesus in seeing His kingdom established here on earth; that includes taking authority over the powers of darkness in ways we may not have thought, in the mundane and practical issues of life.

In order to explore these ideas more fully, we first need to look at the nature of the spiritual world and see how it can interfere with the natural world as we know it.

Chapter 2

Two Dimensions of Battle

The spiritual world is of course unseen by the natural eye. However, we know that this realm is made up of angels, fallen angels (more often referred to as demons or evil spirits) and God, who is ruler over all.

The physical world is more familiar to us, as it is full of material things which we can see and touch, e.g. plant and animal life, hills and rivers. However, God has created man as both a spiritual and a physical being. We read in 1 Thess. 5:23 that man is *"spirit, soul and body."* The following diagram illustrates the resulting situation.

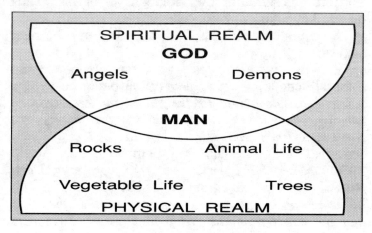

As we can see, man functions in both the spiritual and the physical dimensions. We will, therefore, be affected by the activities which go on in both realms. Whether we like it or not, that *is* the situation.

As human beings we are involved in both the spiritual level and the physical level; Satan knows that as well as God. Our calling as Christians is to help bring in the kingdom of God on earth, i.e. a society based on Biblical principles. Satan's goal is to prevent this from happening[2]. Thus he will interfere on both levels. *That* is the battle we're talking about.

There are many examples of these two levels of spiritual/physical warfare recorded in the history of God's people, Israel. One is found in Exodus chapter seventeen, where Amalek has come to fight with Israel at Rephidim.

Note the strategy decided here. Moses takes Aaron and Hur to the top of a nearby hill where they pray (exercise spiritual authority), while Joshua and his army fight the battle in the valley (exercise physical authority).

Moses, on top of the mountain, cries out to the Lord to intervene in the situation. With his hands raised, he petitions God. He acts as an intercessor, as he stands between the God he serves and the men he leads.

Without doubt this passage shows us how these spiritual actions affected the physical battle below, for *"as long as Moses held up his hands, the Israelites were winning, but whenever he lowered his hands, the Amalekites were winning"* (Exodus 17:11). Both activities were necessary and both were hard work. *"When Moses' hands grew tired, they took a stone and put it under him and he sat on it. Aaron and Hur held his hands up – one on one side, one on the other – so that his hands remained steady until sunset. So Joshua overcame the Amalekite army with the sword"* (Exodus 17:12-13). Work in both levels brought victory to God's people.

Yet this story is not meant just to be enjoyed. Rather, it reveals a principle which God wants us to grasp and use in our daily lives. As I write this I'm reminded of an incident which took place recently, and which was resolved only when the two levels of battle were engaged.

A new sewage system was being installed at the King's Lodge, a 13 acre property which houses our family and 100 other YWAM staff and students. As this would affect all of us in a very practical way, you can imagine that we were all keen that it be a smooth installation. Yet things began to go wrong at the crucial stage of the procedure.

As the huge 3,500 gallon fibreglass sewer container rested in its newly dug hole and was slowly filled up with water, concrete was poured around its outside perimeter. However, instead of the concrete holding the huge container in place, the container began to float, and it then tipped over, so that it was partly stuck in the concrete and partly jutting into the air. This was *not* part of the installation design!

The only thing to do was try and lift the container out and start again, so we arranged for a crane and driver to come the next day. By the time he arrived, the container had been sitting in the concrete for eighteen hours! As he looked at the problem, the crane driver exclaimed, "Oh, not one of these again. I've never seen one of these ever come out whole. They've always broken when we've tried to pull them out." The sewer container was made of fibreglass and was not designed to be lifted while full of water. When filled it weighed around 42 tons! The crane would certainly be stretched to its limit.

At that point the temptation for us as a community was to accept the circumstances and believe the crane driver's comments that the situation was hopeless. However, as the workmen gathered sceptically at the site to attempt their daunting task, a group of staff members decided to gather in an upstairs room to pray.

Recalling the prayer time, Kay said: "We deliberately focused our attention upon the Lord – His power, His might, and His authority. Faith began to rise up in our hearts that God could do the impossible and overrule in the ordinary aspects of life.

One person felt prompted to read Colossians 1:17, which talks about God holding all things together. We then corporately declared the truth of this verse and prayed that the God who held all things together by His word of power would enable the container to be lifted out. We continued to pray fervently until we had the assurance in our hearts that we had received the answer to our prayer by faith, and that God had actually done it in the spiritual realm."

While the group prayed upstairs, down at the working site the crane driver turned on the ignition. As the crane chugged to lift the container free from the concrete cast, small cracks began to appear in the fibreglass. Pieces of wood were then positioned around the container to strengthen it. As the driver raised the arm of his crane, the small group of people standing around the working site all held their breath. But this time the sewer was lifted clear and in one piece! The relief reflected on everyone's face quickly gave way to utter amazement as they realised what had just taken place.

God had held the sewer container together and everyone knew it, even the crane driver. He knew we were a Christian community and that we were praying about the situation. Remembering how regularly his wife went to church, he said to one of our staff, "I think I'll start going to church after what I've seen this morning."

The concrete was then removed and the hole made ready for the sewer container to be reinstalled. We were all aware that "victory" had come when we had followed Moses' example and prayed, while the men were working on the site as Joshua had done.

These two levels of battle (spiritual and physical) also appear in another Old Testament story. In 2 Kings chapter six we read that the king of Aram was at war with Israel. However, as long as the king of Israel obeyed the Lord, as speaking through Elisha the prophet, his army remained undefeated.

When the king of Aram heard about Elisha, he determined to capture him. We then read that *"When the servant of the man of God got up and went out early the next morning, an army with horses and chariots surrounded the city. 'Oh, my lord, what shall we do?' the servant asked. 'Don't be afraid,' the prophet answered. 'Those who are with us are more than those who are with them.' And Elisha prayed, 'Oh Lord, open his eyes that he may see.' Then the Lord opened the servant's eyes, and he looked and saw the hills full of horses and chariots of fire all around Elisha"* (2 Kings 6:15-17).

Here was a situation in which, to the natural eye, the odds looked impossible. It frightened the young man and he began to panic. Elisha remained calm as he saw the situation not only with his natural eyes but also with his spiritual eyes. (Remember, the group praying for the sewer received faith, while some of those in the "valley" remained sceptical.)

Realising that words alone won't combat the young man's fear, Elisha asked the Lord to give him the same spiritual vision. The result was dynamic. As God opened his spiritual eyes to see the array of angelic forces armed for combat, the young man suddenly had a different perspective. His sense of panic subsided and faith, not fear, rose within him.

But, again, this is not meant to be a one-off incident, brushed aside as relevant only to Old Testament times. God still has an army of angels ready to come to the aid of His people in the 21st century. The Bible speaks about God's angels as *"ministering spirits sent to serve those who will inherit salvation"* (Hebrews 1:14). We also read that *"the angel of the Lord encamps around those who fear him, and he delivers them"* (Psalm 34:7). I believe that we witnessed an example of this with our sewer, as God sent His angels to hold it together and deliver it from the ground!

Many of us know what it is like to feel overwhelmed by our circumstances. It may, however, be a new thought that the source of some of these difficulties lie in the spiritual dimension. If this is the case for you, I encourage you to pray and ask the Lord to give you spiritual eyes, as He did for Elisha's servant.

Questions

1. How can we become more aware of the spiritual realm around us?

2. Is there a situation at work, home or school where you need to see with your spiritual eyes?

Chapter 3

Satan's Opposition

I'm convinced that in these days God is trying to awaken us to the whole dimension of spiritual battle. To understand the nature of the battle more fully, we need to look at God's part in the battle with the Christian in partnership, and Satan's part in his opposition to this taking place.

As we begin to consider Satan's role, it's helpful to get clear in our minds the distinction between his *personal* opposition to us as children of God and his *general* opposition to us bringing in the kingdom of God on earth.

In the last chapter we saw an example of Satan's general opposition, in the battle at Rephidim. The Amalekites were opposing the Israelites – the people God had chosen to bring in His kingdom on earth. Yet as Moses recognised the source of the opposition to be spiritual, he was able to take the appropriate action by exercising spiritual authority and the enemy's strategy was confounded.

An example of Satan's personal opposition to us as children of God is seen in the following incident:

As Gillian sat down at the table she accidentally bumped Neil's arm, causing his mug of coffee to spill over the front page of his newspaper. Exploding into anger Neil shouted at her, "Why do you have to be so clumsy?" Feeling dreadfully hurt, Gillian burst into tears while Neil, feeling guilty about his outburst, stomped down the hall into the bedroom.

Throwing himself into the bedside chair Neil inwardly kicked himself. He'd blown it again. Why did he react like that? He was usually an even-tempered man, but recently even the least little thing Gillian did seemed to infuriate him. Why?

Dropping to his knees in desperation, Neil prayed, "Lord, help me." As he knelt there in the silence, memories of his outbursts over the past few days flashed before his mind. Realising that the problem was getting out of control, Neil resolved to talk with one of the church elders.

Several days later Neil and Jim got together. Over coffee Jim asked Neil a few questions about his background, and in the course of his reply Neil revealed that his father was a man who often lost his temper. As a teenager, Neil was often on the receiving end of his father's anger. Sometimes it was justified, but other times it was not. As a result, Neil developed a deep resentment towards his father.

In the moments which followed his reply Neil began to realise the cause of his bottled up anger. Jim waited for a while and then gently asked him, "Have you forgiven your father for the hurt he caused you?" Neil shook his head. Jim then explained that when we focus on our hurt, instead of forgiving the person who hurt us, we grow resentful and bitter. This often expresses itself in anger. Jim went on to say, "as you forgive your father, God is able to release you from your own anger."

For some time Neil sat struggling with an unwillingness to forgive his father. Jim waited, silently praying for him. Eventually, Neil began to pray, "Lord, I'm sorry for my hardness of heart. My father hurt me deeply, but I choose to forgive him now. Please cleanse me from my resentment."

That prayer marked the beginning of freedom for Neil. He went on to ask the Lord's forgiveness for his own anger and later, when he returned home, he humbled himself and asked Gillian to forgive him.

Through this incident we can trace Satan's personal opposition to Neil as a child of God. When Neil was hurt by his father he could have forgiven him (representing God's character in the situation), or he could choose not to forgive him (thwarting the godly development of his own character). Neil's choice not to forgive his father allowed resentment to take root in his heart. And as time passed, and the hurt was unresolved, a stronghold of resentment developed within Neil. This was eventually expressed in his relationship with his wife.

Their marriage relationship was saved from possible disaster by Neil repenting and receiving forgiveness from God and from his wife. While Neil held onto his resentment his problem of anger increased, forming a stronghold of unforgiveness. Repenting and receiving God's forgiveness enabled God to come in and set him free.

It was Neil's initial response which delighted Satan as he could then encourage similar responses to further hurtful experiences. Harbouring unforgiveness in our hearts is one of the most common doorways through which he gains an influence in our lives and creates a stronghold. Satan's opposition is towards us personally (as children of God his motive is to thwart our growth in godliness) and generally (opposing the advancement of the kingdom of God on earth). As we continue to consider the nature of the battle it will be helpful to keep this personal/general distinction in mind.

Remember also that the only reason for considering Satan's role in the battle is to understand how he operates, so we can plan to counteract his strategies. Our purpose is not to acquire more factual knowledge but to engage in active training.

Part of the training for many heavy-weight boxers is to watch videos of their opponent's previous fights. Why? — to study every move an opponent makes, what his main punches are, and where his weaknesses lie. He can then form an intelligent plan of attack for the next fight. In the same way we need to make ourselves aware of the enemy's tactics.

In Ephesians 6:11 Paul exhorts us to *"Put on the full armour of God so that you can take your stand against the devil's schemes."* Note that the word "schemes" is plural, indicating that the devil has more than one trick up his sleeve. An alternative translation for schemes is "crafty deceptions." Not only does the devil have many plans, but they are crafty and full of deception.

In fact one of the names for the devil is deceiver! What does the deception involve? In many instances it signifies a distortion of truth. Therefore from this one verse we already have some insight as to how the devil will operate. He will seek to twist truth in our eyes, and he is crafty in such methods.

From the beginning of our history we see that Satan has understood the power of distorting truth. If we look at the scene in the garden of Eden, recorded in Genesis chapter three, Satan does not immediately suggest to Eve that she eat the fruit from the tree which God had placed out of bounds. That would be too obvious. No, he's more subtle and instead questions God's motives for giving such an instruction. He distorts the truth and entices her to believe that God does not have her best interests at heart.

When Eve listens to Satan's reasoning, rather than

holding fast to what God specifically said, she begins to believe a lie and so chooses to disobey God. She then influences Adam, and he too deliberately disobeys God and Satan's trick works. Their disobedience gives him authority to influence their thinking and actions as a couple. Since that time Satan's success rate in other people's lives has been phenomenal, as they in turn have chosen to disobey God.

We can therefore see that Satan's behaviour in the garden of Eden sets the stage for his actions throughout history. Although he is subtle in his tactics, nevertheless he does reveal his underlying motive – i.e. to entice people like you and me to listen to lies and act accordingly.

Keeping this in mind, let's look at some of Satan's other schemes.

Questions

1. What is an example of Satan's personal opposition in your life?

2. Think of some of the ways Satan seeks to bring general opposition to the body of Christ.

3. How can we break free from his opposition?

Chapter 4

Satan's Schemes

There are many references in Scripture to the activities of Satan. We read that Satan opposes God's work (1 Thessalonians 2:18); hinders the Gospel (Matthew 13:19, 2 Corinthians 4:4); blinds, deceives and ensnares the wicked (Luke 22:3, Revelation 20:78, 1 Timothy 3:7); afflicts (Job 1:2) and tempts the saints of God (1 Timothy 3:5).

Just a note of caution at this point, to avoid elevating Satan and making him bigger than he is. Although he is powerful, he is not all powerful. And he doesn't roam free with evil; he's restricted by God. This is evident in the book of Job.

At the beginning of the book, Job becomes the focus of a heavenly conversation between God and Satan. Held up as a model of godly devotion and worship, Job's faithfulness to God is attacked by Satan as being based on Job's financial prosperity. *"But stretch out your hand and strike everything he has,"* Satan accuses, *"and he will surely curse you to your face"* (Job 1:11). God responds to this accusation by permitting Satan to destroy everything which belongs to Job; yet He puts a hedge of protection around Job himself.

From this situation it's evident that Satan's activities in this universe are limited by God. Only with God's permission (and with divinely imposed limitations) can he exercise some power. It's in this context that we'll consider two questions: firstly, how does Satan seek to exercise power in our world as we know it, and secondly, how does that affect us in our everyday situations?

Let's look at some of Satan's activities and apply them to our own lives: –

Discouragement

Consider the following strategy planning council:

Satan called a meeting of his servants to talk about how they could make a good man sin. One demon said, "I'll make him sin by setting the pleasures of sin before him. I'll tell him of sin's delights and the rich rewards it brings." "That won't work," said Satan. "He's tried sin and knows better than that." Then another demon said, "I'll make him sin by telling him of the pains and sorrows of virtue. I'll show him that virtue has no delights and brings no rewards." "That won't do either," cried Satan, "for he walks in virtue and knows Wisdom's ways are *'pleasant ways, and all her paths are peace'*" (Proverbs 3:17). "Well", said another demon, "I'll make him sin by discouraging his soul." "Ah, that will do it!" cried Satan. "We'll conquer him now!"

Each one of us experiences times of discouragement. For example, we may have spent a lot of time and energy working on a project, only to discover at the last minute that an alteration in plans meant it needed to be handled in a completely different way. Maybe we've sat an examination, only to walk away knowing that we didn't answer the questions very well. Or it could be that we've worked hard at our job and yet received no recognition for it. At such times it's natural to feel discouraged and at this point our response is crucial. Will we be honest with the

Lord about how we feel and receive His affirmation,[3] or will we yield to the temptation to give up? If we choose the latter response, we give the enemy a foothold in our lives, which then gives him the opportunity to attack us through discouragement. Let me give you an example.

Lisa was the mother of three pre-school children. Having them at home with her all day meant she led an extremely busy life. Amongst other things her daily routine included picking up the kid's clothes, wiping their noses, endless loads of washing, ironing, cooking meals and so on.

After one particularly discouraging day Lisa felt worn out. In her weariness she began to think back with longing to the time when she didn't have children. These thoughts were reinforced as she recalled the seemingly carefree life of the single people in her street. Instead of expressing how she felt to the Lord and receiving His strength and perspective, Lisa continued to compare herself unfavourably with others. As a result she was irritable with her husband and children and the days which followed never seemed to end.

By dwelling on the mundaneness of her daily life, Lisa gave the devil a doorway into her mind. As she focused on the negative aspects Lisa lost sight of the responsibility God had given her to develop the potential in her children. This was just what the devil wanted to happen. He knows the powerful influence mothers have, not only to train their children to be responsible adults but also to disciple them, that they might know the Lord and walk in His ways. But he also knows that a powerful way to prevent this happening is through persistent discouragement.

Anxiety

One dictionary definition of anxiety is "a painful uneasiness of mind about an impending or anticipated problem."

We all face anxious periods from time to time – students preparing for exams, businessmen encountering a pressured situation at work, unemployed people worrying about how to pay the next food bill . . . Yet the devil's desire is to see that these natural concerns develop into a grip by which he holds us and won't allow us a moment's peace.

Several years ago I suffered a period of anxiety. I'd been appointed as leader of one of our YWAM bases in the U.K. – a role which involved a lot of responsibility. There were a lot of things on my mind, so when I started to have trouble sleeping I put it down to the newness of increased responsibility. My sleeplessness continued night after night. I'd wake up in the middle of the night, completely alert. Thoughts of all the things I needed to do would crowd into my mind, making further sleep impossible. Or so I thought!

In desperation I asked the Lord if there was something I needed to do to get rid of the anxiety. Then in my daily Bible reading I came across the words, *"Cast all your anxiety on him because he cares for you"* (1 Peter 5:7). I realised that the way to break the gripping effect of my anxiety each night was to commit all my responsibilities to the Lord *before* going to sleep. As I began putting the above scripture into practice, I eventually slept peacefully throughout the night. The hold that the devil had gained on my mind through anxiety was broken when I committed my concerns to the Lord first, instead of trying to struggle with them in the middle of the night.

Division

In any relationship – whether it be marriage, friendship, family, work or church – disagreements will occur. This is natural and is not necessarily wrong. The important thing is how we handle such disagreements. Do we agree to differ and yet remain in unity, or do we allow our disagreements to lead to division?

On one occasion Jesus spoke to the Pharisees, saying *"Every kingdom divided against itself will not stand"* (Matthew 12:25). One of the goals of the enemy is to cause division. He will therefore tempt us to stubbornly hold onto our own opinion during a disagreement, so that a wall of separation arises and prevents us from relating as we should.

One of the basic issues involved in division is, of course, pride. It is expressed in an unwillingness to hear the other's point of view, not wanting to let your opinion go. The result is that we become locked into our own perspective and the devil blinds us to the root of our problem.

For example, I was recently counselling a married couple who were having problems with unresolved conflicts. Initially they'd had a difference of opinion about an issue and began judging each other, rather than attempting to reach an agreement. This was just the ground the devil needed to cause serious division between them. He then began to fill the husband's mind with accusing thoughts about his wife. It soon got to the stage where the husband believed these accusations to be true and spoke them out to his wife. Utterly devastated, the wife burst into tears.

When I suggested to the husband that there seemed to be a spirit of division interfering with their marriage on the basis of his accusation, he realised what had happened and asked his wife to forgive him. She forgave her husband and then we prayed together, the husband beginning to resist the devil, instead of resisting his wife.[4] Breaking down the spiritual wall was the first step to resolving their conflicts!

A similar wall can develop between parents and children with the so-called "generation gap." Once again it involves people sticking to their point of view, being unwilling to yield and seek a common solution with which both parties are happy. Sometimes the immaturity of the child can make this difficult, but it's not always the case.

Compromise

Another devilish scheme is compromise, which is often reflected in our lifestyle. How does he do this? A common tactic is to influence us to live according to two sets of standards: one set for use at home and church and one set for our place of work.

For example, the devil won't mind if we profess our Christianity openly in a church service as long as we compromise our standards at work. He realises that if the words we speak are not reflected in our actions then we are hypocrites!

How does the devil tempt us to compromise? Some of the common temptations are to take shortcuts or to be involved in underhand methods at work (pilfering, cheating, blackmail and so forth). Or he may tempt us to work excessive hours of overtime – encouraging our desire to provide material goods for our children, at the expense of quality time with our family. Whatever the situation if we try to live according to two sets of standards, Satan has successfully established a stronghold of compromise in our lives.

Confusion

The devil is well aware of the destructive effect of confusion in our lives. He therefore makes much use of this scheme; one of his main targets being your children.

Children are often confused between values they are taught at home and those to which they're exposed at school. We have learnt with our children not to immediately assume that angry outbursts or absent-mindedness are due to rebellion or carelessness. It may be necessary to probe further about what has happened at school that day. If they've been in a situation where the standards have conflicted with those taught at home, they will have experienced tension and confusion. When back at home, faced with different values, the children can feel confused and express this through anger or absent-mindedness.

Fear

We all have natural fears: snakes, wasps, earthquakes and so on. However, the devil seeks to see people gripped by unnatural fears, e.g. fear of the dark, fear of failure, fear of what people may think of us.

Moses was a classic Biblical example of the fear of man. When the Lord commissioned Moses to lead his people out of Egypt, his first response was *"Who am I?"*, followed by, *"Oh Lord, I have never been eloquent, neither in the past nor since you have spoken to your servant. I am slow of speech and tongue"* (Exodus 4:10). His eyes were focused too much on what others would think of him, together with his own inadequacies.

Kay used to have a similar struggle. As we talked

about it recently she said, "I had a real fear of talking to people I didn't know. I didn't know how to open up a conversation – but even if I could, I was afraid they'd think I was stupid!

This fear wasn't something I faced only once in a while, but every day, as I stood at the same bus stop with the same people. And as each day went by the struggle within me grew more intense, i.e. 'I ought to . . . but I can't.' I'm scared of making a fool of myself.

It was one day as I was reading my Bible that I realised this fear of man was in fact sin! In 2 Timothy 1:7 it says, *"For God did not give us a spirit of timidity, but a spirit of power, of love and of self-discipline."* By dwelling on what others would think of me I'd allowed the enemy to develop a stronghold of fear in my life. It was only as I repented of the fear and began to receive the Lord's encouragement that I started to have confidence in initiating conversations."

Obviously the above list of examples is not exhaustive. However, my aim is to arouse an awareness of Satan's activity in this world and to inspire us to a greater level of alertness in our own lives.

Questions

1. Do you recognise any of Satan's schemes mentioned in this chapter?

2. Identify some of Satan's other schemes.

Chapter 5

God's Character

Having considered Satan's nature, together with some of his temptations in our world, let's turn our attention to the nature and character of God.

In Jeremiah 51:15 we read,

> *"He made the earth by his power;*
> *he founded the world by his wisdom*
> *and stretched out the heavens by his*
> *understanding."* [5]

What a contrast between Satan's nature and the nature of God! Whereas Satan is a created, finite being (and a fallen one at that!) God is uncreated and infinite in power. He is the One who created all things.

To create, God had only to speak a word and the planets were formed in the heavens. Stars were likewise set in space not haphazardly but in constellations. And into the Milky Way Galaxy He placed the earth.

On this Earth God moulded the mountains and hills, arranged rock formations, and breathed life into the soil. Fruit trees and cedars, flowering plants and thorn bushes appeared.

Separating the continents from each other, He then poured water into the oceans and filled them with animal life. As on the land, the sea yielded endless varieties of life forms, each species able to survive and reproduce in unique ways.

The marks of the Designer are evident in the heavens and the earth. In every part of this design we see God's unlimited resources of creativity and power. Furthermore, as we saw in chapter one, *"in Him all things hold together"* (Colossians 1:17). Not only has God created all things but He is the One who sustains all things. Only He has *all* power. Therefore, it's clear that if the battle between God and Satan depended on sheer power, God could easily win!

Yet God does not rule by power alone. Jeremiah also refers to His wisdom and understanding. Along with His power, God's wisdom is eternal. It is perfect, immediate (not gained through experience or developed over time), true and with purpose.[6]

God's wisdom and understanding is also revealed in creation. For example, I was reading in a magazine that the earth is approximately 93 million miles away from the sun. Scientists tell us that if we were 120 million miles away we'd freeze. Yet if we were only 60 million miles away we'd be burnt out! Once again the contrast between Satan and God is marked. Whereas Satan, who only has *some* power, uses it destructively, God not only has *all* power but uses it wisely and with understanding.

God's nature is uncreated. He is eternal and has infinite power, wisdom and understanding. These attributes can be clearly seen in the world around us. Likewise, we can recognise God's true character by considering how He chooses to demonstrate His nature. Instead of holding all things together from a distance, God chose to become involved with His creation. As Francis Schaeffer said, He is the "personal-infinite God." Nowhere is this more evident than in God's creation of you and me.

The fact that we've been made in His own image and likeness (in the sense that God is Spirit) demonstrates the value He places on us.[7] It also reveals His intention that we would relate together, being relaxed in each other's presence, knowing acceptance and trust. In other words He did not want to rule us by force but seeks to have a relationship based on love. (N.B. God's love has never been based solely on emotions which can come and go; He consistently makes the highest and best choices for the human race.)

Initially, God's desire for close relationship with man was fulfilled. We read in the early chapters of Genesis that not only was God pleased with everything He'd made, but also His relationship with Adam and Eve was going well. In fact, it's clear that their relationship was very open. We read in Genesis 3:8a, *"Then the man and his wife heard the sound of the Lord God as he was walking in the garden in the cool of the day . . . "* This is a picture of intimacy. God did not distance Himself from His creation; He walked and talked with Adam and Eve, sharing His knowledge with them. (This is in complete contrast to Satan who likes to keep things hidden and to deceive and distort the truth.).

The situation did not remain as God intended for very long. In chapter three Satan, in his conversation with Eve, attempts to malign God's character. He sows a seed of doubt in her mind: *"Does God really care about you? Isn't He really after His own interests?"*

As Eve begins to dwell upon this innuendo, she and then Adam make the decision to reject God's command. As a result, their relationship with God is no longer open and natural. Instead of acceptance and trust, Adam and Eve now know guilt, fear and shame.

Yet how does God respond? If, as Satan suggests, He doesn't care, then we can expect Him to react to their rebellion by wiping out the entire human race! Why bother with people who won't co-operate?

Instead we see a God who will not give up on His people! He still wants to have a relationship with them. Therefore He looks for a way to redeem the situation so that once more their relationship can be based on love and truth. His solution, when it was carried out, demonstrated the depth of His love for us.

Before we consider the implications of this solution, let's pause for a moment. Recalling the scene in the garden, imagine Satan, gloating triumphantly as he watches the departing figures of Adam and Eve. Now try to sense the anguish of God for those He loves, as He is honour bound to follow through with the consequences of their sin-death. Why is the situation so serious? To answer this, we need to consider another aspect of God's nature: His holiness!

So comprehensive is the attribute of holiness in reference to God's nature that it's even emphasized in the repetition of His title, i.e. *"Holy, holy, holy, is the Lord God Almighty, who was, and is, and is to come"* (Revelation 4:8).

Holiness is not something God has; God *is* holy. To be holy is to be set apart; to be separate from sin. The Anglo-Saxon root word of holy is "hal", meaning "whole". He does not compromise with anything contrary to His nature. Rather, He is set apart from sin and is completely whole.

God's plan was that we would enjoy wholeness too. However, as Adam and Eve chose to disobey God, their sin caused a whole separation between them and God; a separation which Satan relished.

Yet Satan's glee was short lived. At immense cost to Himself, God provided the solution which satisfied the demands of justice and also allowed for mercy. The holiness of God is the ground or basis of both His justice and His love. The justice of God must punish sin; the love of God wants to forgive sin. Both of these are properly kept in balance as God's holiness forms the basis of His actions. As Strong has stated, "The holiness of God is the track upon which the train of His love runs".[8]

Through the implementation of His plan, God's true character is clearly revealed for all to see. As Jesus was born into the human race and grew up, experiencing everything that any other person faces, He showed us it's not only possible to obey God, but also demonstrated by His own life what God is like. The results were plain. Crowds gathered around Him wherever He went; they hungrily took in all His words. The sick were made well. Down-and-outers were given hope. Children felt free to play and draw close to Him.

Throughout His years on earth Jesus consistently pointed His hearers to God the Father. In John 14:8-9 we read: *"Philip said, 'Lord, show us the Father and that will be enough for us'. Jesus answered, 'Don't you know me, Philip, even after I have been among you such a long time? Anyone who has seen me has seen the Father."*

An example of Jesus reflecting the Father's character can be seen in the story of the woman caught in adultery (see John 8:1-11). The Pharisees deliberately put Jesus in an awkward position. If He dealt with the situation as the law of Moses demanded, Jesus would be accused of being harsh. However, if He let the woman go free, He would be accused of weakness.

What did Jesus do? He both challenged the Pharisees (*"If any one of you is without sin, let him be the first to throw a stone at her"*) and then spoke to the woman in such a way that was neither harsh nor compromising, (*"Neither do I condemn you. Go now and leave your life of sin"*). Jesus was totally compassionate in His approach to the woman, not condemning her, and yet not condoning her sin either.

By His very life and death Jesus showed us the loving character of God. He also demonstrated His power over Satan. Whenever Jesus encountered demonic powers He simply commanded them to go – and they had no choice but to leave! Nothing could withstand His power.

Let's look at an example of this in Mark's Gospel. A desperate father brought his son to Jesus for help. Since childhood this boy had a history of violent seizures and convulsions. The father pleaded with Jesus to heal his son. How did Jesus respond? He rebuked the evil spirit, saying, *"You deaf and mute spirit, I command you, come out of him and never enter him again,"* and the spirit immediately left him. Jesus then took him by the hand and lifted him to his feet and he stood up (Mark 9:25-7). When Jesus met with demonic powers His authority was clear and decisive and the evil spirits could not withstand it. The "gates of hell" shall "hold no power over" the church's cornerstone, Jesus Christ!

When Jesus rose from the dead He conquered the power of sin. As we come to God through the atoning death of Jesus, He then gives us *His* power to stand up and fight!

In order that we might really understand this power available to us as 21st century Christians living in partnership with God we need to look at what happened on the Cross and ask the question: "How did Jesus defeat the devil?"

Questions:

1. In what other ways do we see God the Father revealed in Jesus' life on earth?

2. How has God been consistent with His character in your life?

MEDITATE on the following words of a contemporary chorus:

"You are the mighty God
   Ruler of the worlds You've made
You are the living God
   The great I AM
You are the holy One,
   Perfect in purity
You are the Lord of all
   Yet You've called me Your friend"

Chapter 6

God's Victory

When Jesus hung on the Cross, to all appearances having failed in His mission, He was in fact carrying out His greatest task; a task which would impact the lives of billions of people.

Up until this point in history men and women had tried numerous ways to get rid of the guilt of their sin, but none had worked. The nearest solution appeared to be the animal sacrifices, practiced yearly in Old Testament times on the Day of Atonement.[9] Although these sacrifices brought home to people the seriousness of their sin, the fact that they were repeated year after year shows us that in themselves they were not enough to atone for sin once and for all. In the New Testament, however, we read that, *"Christ died for sins once and for all, the righteous for the unrighteous, to bring you to God"* (1 Peter 3:18).

In complete contrast to the animal sacrifices of past generations, the effectiveness of the Cross is seen in the fact that Jesus was able to take into His own body the sin and punishment for sin of everyone in the world – past, present and future.[10] Jesus, the sinless Son of God, became sin for us.[11]

Yet the power of the Cross lies not only in the fact that Jesus bore our sins, but that He did so completely alone. As long as Jesus carried our sins in His body, God could not look upon Him and had to turn away. Why? In the last chapter we briefly

35

touched on the holiness of God and saw that holiness means to be separate from sin. Therefore, God in His holiness could not look upon the sin that had been laid on His own Son.

From Jesus's point of view this separation from His Father was far worse that the physical pain He was suffering. How can we know that? The Gospel accounts reveal that up until the time of the crucifixion Jesus was in such close relationship with God that He continually talked to Him and referred to Him personally as "Father". Yet on the Cross the enormity of the separation which took place as He bore our sins was such that He cried out: *"My God, my God, why have You forsaken me?"*[12] This was the only time that Jesus prayed and didn't address God as "Father."

However, so that our image of God doesn't become distorted at this point, we need to keep in perspective the understanding which we have of His character so far. We've noted that every thought and act of God has been motivated by love. We've also realised that He is holy and therefore cannot condone sin. We can understand some of the anguish God must have felt as Adam and Eve disobeyed Him and departed from the garden. With all this in mind, try to imagine the intensity of the Father's anguish during Jesus' crucifixion. For at this time the sin which Jesus took upon Himself created a barrier, so that He couldn't see or feel God's presence. This separation was the real agony of the Cross!

Yet this temporary separation was in itself the final death blow to the power of sin. As Jesus' final moments are recorded by John we read, *"When He had received the drink, Jesus said, 'It is finished'. With that, He bowed His head and gave up His spirit"* (John 19:30).

In the Greek, the words "It is finished" are translated, "tetelesthai," a cry of triumph meaning "finished" or "accomplished". There was nothing more to be done! (In the Greek market place fishmongers would stamp "tetelesthai" on the customer's receipt, to verify that "it has been paid".)

As Jesus voluntarily surrendered His spirit to God, He did so with the confidence that the power over sin was broken.

Atonement had been made once and for all. The gruesomeness of the yearly sacrifice was no longer necessary. Jesus' atoning sacrifice was sufficient. Jesus truly is our redeemer!

Yet the death of Jesus is only one side of the Cross. After Jesus bore our sin and died we read that God raised Him from the dead. Death could not keep its hold on Jesus.[13] The resurrection is the other side of the Cross. It is the "Amen" of the Father to the voluntary sacrifice of Jesus the Son.

Where does this leave Satan? In Colossians we read that *"having disarmed the powers and authorities, He (Jesus) made a public spectacle of them, triumphing over them by the cross"* (Colossians 2:15).

As Paul is writing to fellow Roman citizens, he uses an example from his own culture to illustrate what Jesus accomplished on the Cross. His readers would recall the pomp and pageantry of the victorious procession along the main street of Rome after a battle had been won. At the head of the procession the victorious general would drive his chariot towards the emperor to receive his welcome and reward, while tied to his chariot, stripped of his armour and in chains, the defeated general and his soldiers would be dragged along in the dust.

The picture is quite graphic and is a good one for Paul to use to illustrate the effectiveness of the

Cross. If we imagine God as the emperor and Jesus as the victorious general, riding home in victory and dragging Satan and his demons behind him, we begin to get a true perspective of Satan's position – disarmed and in chains! Again, holding no power over the church.

From the beginning, Satan had gained authority in people's lives only through their sin. On the Cross Jesus struck the death blow to sin. Satan has not, however, been entirely removed from the scene! He still *"prowls around like a roaring lion looking for someone to devour"* (1 Peter 5:8). Although Satan is disarmed he is not annihilated, which means we still need to deal with him in this world.

It is only as we choose to turn from all known sin in our lives and submit to the lordship of Jesus that Satan will be rendered powerless in our lives.[14] Satan will continue to remain powerless in our lives as long as we don't give him a foothold through further sin. The following incident is a good analogy:

Several years ago I was staying with a friend whose house was being invaded by flies. After questioning our neighbours to see if they were experiencing the same problem we found that our house was the only one, so we began searching the property for any likely cause of the pests.

Eventually Jim discovered a rubbish bag, full of kitchen refuse. It had obviously been left there for weeks, as inside the bag was a seething mass of maggots!

Gingerly picking up the offensive bag, Jim immediately put it in the boot of his car and drove to the dump. Having disposed of the rubbish, he returned home to find that within a short time the problem of the flies was solved.

Interestingly enough, one of Satan's names is

"Beelzebub," which means "Prince of the Flies." However, if we take the analogy further, Jim knew that he wouldn't solve the problem of the flies by attacking them with a can of spray; he needed to deal with the source of corruption on which they were feeding and multiplying.[15] In a similar way, when we want to deal with the enemy we won't get very far by chasing demons; but we will if we remove the source of corruption in our lives: unconfessed sin.

In chapter four we considered some of the many ways Satan will influence us to give him authority in our lives. We need to learn to be alert to his schemes so that we don't sin. If we find it difficult to gain victory over the enemy in a particular area, one of the first things to check is whether there is unconfessed sin in our lives. Secondly, we need to make sure we've given the area of struggle to the Lord Jesus.

Maintaining the lordship of Christ in our lives is vital if we are to see the devil defeated in our own lives as well as to actively work in partnership with God, to see His kingdom come on earth. In the book of Ephesians, where Paul gives us a strategy to oppose the devil, he uses the analogy of a soldier preparing for physical battle in the light of Christians preparing for spiritual battle. We will consider this strategy in more detail in the rest of this book. However, at this point it's important to realise that the pieces of armour, which Paul mentions, actually reflect aspects of Jesus' character. For us to be effective in this battle our character needs to reflect the character of Jesus. How will we reflect Jesus' character? By obeying Him as Lord on a daily basis.

Questions:

1. What did Jesus' death on the Cross achieve for you and me?

2. What did the Cross mean for Satan and his demons?

3. How can we prevent Satan from gaining any authority in our lives?

SECTION TWO:
"STAND FIRM"

Chapter 7

Power To Stand

You and I are involved in a spiritual battle! Whether we like it or not that is the situation. As General William Booth (founder of the Salvation Army) once said, "There is no discharge in this war." The question is, will we affect it or will it affect us?

Jesus shows us how we can affect the battle! During His life on earth He demonstrated His strategy not only for overcoming the devil's influence in His life, but also for affecting the battle in the spiritual and physical realms. In Ephesians six, Paul sums up this strategy. He encourages Christians to overcome the devil's influence in their lives and help bring in the kingdom of God on earth.

To communicate this message, Paul uses the analogy between a soldier putting on his armour in readiness for battle and a Christian reflecting aspects of Jesus' character in the face of opposition by the devil. As we consider the armour and weapons, remember that they are used as an "analogy." Paul is not literally saying that each day we should mentally picture ourselves getting dressed in our spiritual armour; rather, he's exhorting us to reflect aspects of Christ's character in our daily lives.

In Ephesians 6:10-11 Paul writes, *"Be strong in the Lord and in His mighty power. Put on the full armour of God so that you can take your stand against the devil's schemes."* His first concern is that we receive the Lord's strength, rather than rely on our own resources. Paul realises that Christians cannot be effective in opposing Satan unless they're empowered by the Spirit of God. His understanding had certainly been gained through personal experience.

Paul knew full well the results of doing things in his own strength. Before his conversion experience, and convinced of the rightness of his actions, he zealously persecuted those who followed Jesus.[16] As the result of his encounter with the Lord on the road to Damascus, however, Paul was brought to a place of weakness in himself. The Biblical account says, *"when he opened his eyes he could see nothing. So they led him by the hand into Damascus. For three days he was blind, and did not eat or drink anything"* (Acts 9:8-9).

After three days of feeling helpless and probably quite humiliated, the scriptures tell us that *"Ananias went to the house and entered it. Placing his hands on Saul (who was later called Paul), he said, 'Brother Saul, the Lord – Jesus, who appeared to you on the road as you were coming here – has sent me so that you may see again and be filled with the Holy Spirit.' Immediately, something like scales fell from Saul's eyes, and he could see again"* (Acts 9:17-18). Not only did he regain his physical sight, but Paul now yielded to the lordship of Jesus and he was filled with the Holy Spirit. The account goes on to record that after this experience he *" began to preach in the synagogue that Jesus is the Son of God . . . Saul grew more and more powerful and baffled the Jews living in Damascus by proving that Jesus is the Christ"* (Acts 9:20,22).

Paul, or Saul as he was then known, needed to come to a place of weakness in himself, so that he would cease depending on his own strength and instead, become dependent upon God's power.

Likewise, each one of us need to have an encounter with the Holy Spirit. We won't all experience this empowering in the same way. For some it may be a dramatic crisis, as with Paul. For others, like myself, it may be less dramatic but nevertheless a life changing experience. Whatever the nature of our experience, the important thing is that we exchange our weakness for the Lord's mighty power.

My own experience was that I'd been a committed Christian for three years before realising the importance of being filled with the Spirit. When I gave my life to Christ a definite change took place. I knew my sins were forgiven and I had the peace of Jesus in my heart. Yet even though I had the life of the Spirit within me, I lacked His mighty power.

When I tried to communicate the reality of salvation to others nothing seemed to happen. I wasn't getting through to people. (As far as I know, nobody ever gave their life to the Lord as a result of my witness during those first three years!) And in my personal relationship with the Lord there was a lack of intimacy and depth. I had regular quiet times but I knew there should be more reality in my relationship with Him.

Frustrated with my own fruitlessness I began studying the scriptures more intently and discovered many references to people being empowered by the Holy Spirit. I read that Jesus, before beginning His ministry, was filled with the Spirit.[17] (He needed to be strong in His God and the power of His might before He could be effective in dealing with Satan's opposition.) Jesus then instructed His disciples to follow His example: "*Do not leave Jerusalem, but wait for the gift my Father promised, which you have heard me speak about . . . you will receive power when the*

Holy Spirit comes on you; and you will be my witnesses in Jerusalem, and in all Judea and Samaria, and to the ends of the earth" (Acts 1:4,8).

As I read further in the book of Acts it was clear to me that not only were the disciples empowered by the Holy Spirit, as they waited in Jerusalem,[18] but that this experience was intended for *all* who would become disciples of Jesus. As Paul later prayed for the church at Ephesus he said, *"I pray that out of His glorious riches He the Father may strengthen you with power through His Spirit in your inner being, so that Christ may dwell in your hearts through faith"* (Ephesians 3:16-17a).

Listening to other Christians telling me about their experiences of being filled with the Holy Spirit, together with reading books on the subject, further convinced me that this is the desire of God for each one of us. So I asked some friends to pray for me.

Nothing dramatic happened as they prayed, nor did I feel any different, but in the next few weeks my Bible readings became more real to me. In fact, the book of Colossians started to come alive in a new way, especially when I read, *"Christ in you, the hope of glory"* (Colossians 1:27b). For the first time I began to realise the amazing truth that Christ lived in me!

Although I didn't immediately connect this new understanding of the scriptures with my friends' prayers for me to be filled with the Holy Spirit, I gradually became aware that this was what had happened. My experience had certainly not been as dramatic as Paul's, but it was a life changing one. I found it much easier to talk to the Lord in prayer, and He became more real to me when I studied the Bible.

It was several years later that God began to show

me the nature of the spiritual battle and the necessity of me being active in my stand against the devil. But it was so important that before attempting to fight in the battle I needed to be filled with His mighty power. Not only did I need to deepen my intimacy with God in order to understand His character and His ways, but I also needed to receive His power to stand against the devil's schemes.

It is the empowering of the Holy Spirit that Paul refers to when he exhorts us to *"be strong in the Lord and in the power of His might."* And as A. Skevington Wood says, the word used in this verse for "power" is the *"same power that raised Jesus from the dead* (Ephesians 1:20) *and brought them to life when they were dead in trespasses and sin"* (Ephesians 2:1). Its adequacy cannot possibly be in doubt".[19]

God wants each one of us to know the adequacy of His power in and through our lives. He is well aware that we won't affect the spiritual battle in our own strength. In fact, if we try, the battle will affect us! As we've already seen, when we compare the devil with God, the devil is very limited. But when we compare the devil with ourselves, in our human frailty, he is very powerful indeed. We cannot hope to be effective in opposing the enemy unless we are filled, and are continually being filled, with the Holy Spirit.[20]

Jesus, full of the Holy Spirit, was able to stand firm against the temptation of Satan and to oppose his schemes. The early disciples knew what it was to be empowered by the same Spirit that filled Jesus. We can also be filled by the Holy Spirit and affect the spiritual battle by standing firm against Satan's temptations and advancing the kingdom of God. We will be filled with the Holy Spirit when, like Paul, we come to a place where we acknowledge our own weakness and ask for the Lord's power and strength to stand.

Questions

1. Why do we need the empowering of the Holy Spirit?

2. Is there an area in your life where you're trying to do things in your own strength?

3. How do you think you can receive the fullness of the Holy Spirit?

Chapter 8

Stand on Truth

Having established that we need the Lord's strength, Paul considers the individual pieces of armour. His aim is to stimulate our thinking as Christians, so that we'll begin to understand how to oppose the devil.

The first piece of armour specifically mentioned in Ephesians six is the belt of truth. In Roman times the belt was a very important part of the soldier's armour. Not only was the sword attached to the belt, but also the breastplate was hooked onto it. In fact, the soldier's belt was foundational to the rest of his armour.

Paul uses this image to remind us that our commitment to truth is foundational to our spiritual progress as Christians. It is not enough to make an initial response to the *"word of truth, the gospel of your salvation"* (Ephesians 1:13). God is wanting us to develop a commitment to truth in all that we think, say and do. As David says to the Lord, *"Surely you desire truth in the inner parts"* (Psalm 51:6).

At this point it might be helpful to pause and ask, "What is my commitment to truth like? Am I committed to live by the truth without wavering, or am I easily swayed when circumstances get tough?" Let me highlight two major areas where we will be tempted to waver in our commitment to truth.

The first area involves our commitment to the truth about God's loving character. As we've seen in the encounter with Adam and Eve, Satan's initial attack was to question God's character: "Is God who he says he is, and will he do what he says he will do?" Satan was tempting Adam and Eve to waver in their commitment to the truth which they knew about God, and then to actively disobey Him. And as we know, Satan succeeded in his plan of attack.

Satan also tempts us with that same question at various times. He does not give up his attack on God's character just because we've made an initial commitment to truth. On the contrary, he continually tempts us to slacken our belt – usually during times of difficulty.

I remember talking with a Christian young man who had been made unemployed. In his struggles with disappointment and feelings of failure, as well as finding it difficult to find other employment, Satan whispered the thought into Simon's mind, "*If* God really loved you He wouldn't have let this happen."

Instead of refusing to think about this suggestion, realising it to be a lie from the devil, Simon allowed the thought to remain in his mind. He therefore wavered in his commitment to the truth about God's loving character.

As Satan continued to feed similar thoughts into Simon's mind, he began to dwell on them, allowing them to influence his emotions. In doing so, he was indulging in self-pity. As this became a habit pattern for Simon, a stronghold of self-pity began to form in his mind and at this point he yielded his commitment to the truth he knew about God.

Simon, like so many people going through difficult circumstances, needed to realise that God was not to blame for his unemployment. This needed to be settled in his heart and mind. He then needed to recognise that any thoughts which suggested God was to blame were in fact lies from the devil.

After some discussion about this, Simon recognised that Satan had successfully been whispering lies into his mind. He repented of his self-pity and asked God to forgive him for believing lies about His character. He then asked Jesus, who is the truth, to reign in his life once again. In doing so, Simon re-established his commitment to the truth about God's loving-kindness. After he put on the belt of truth in this way God became more real to him as a God of love, a God who was intimately involved with the struggles he was going through. A short time later Simon did get a job.

For each of us, as well as Simon, it's crucial that in our innermost being we consistently affirm the truth that God is who He says He is, and does what He says He will do. In a world where the common cry is "If God is a god of love, *why* . . . ?" we need to be people who direct the blame to its proper source, i.e. sinful man plus the work of Satan. God is a good God and we need to proclaim that with confidence!

The second major area where we'll be tempted to waver in our commitment to truth concerns our identity: "Who am I?" We can choose either to believe what God says about us, or to believe the distorted viewpoints of others.

God established our identity at creation when He made men and women in His own image (i.e. we are spiritual beings). God did not put His Spirit into the trees, plants or animals. Yet he created Adam and Eve with a spirit, soul and body, so that they could have a relationship with Him. They were the only part of God's creation that was made according to His image and likeness – and His response was, *"It was very good"* (Genesis 1:31).

Likewise, each one of us is made in the image of God. The mark of the Creator is upon us. As Francis Schaeffer said, "Man is fallen but he's great." You and I can declare with confidence that we have value because out of all God's creation we are made in His image and likeness.

Yet millions of people, and many Christians too, are ignorant of where their true value lies. They too easily accept the world's value system.

A strong belief held by much of the world is that a person's value depends upon their outward appearance. For example, a beautiful model is admired by the world, earns a lot of money and gets publicity because of her looks. Yet the Bible says, *"The Lord does not look at the things man looks at. Man looks at the outward appearance, but the Lord looks and the heart"* (1 Samuel 16:7b).

Another worldly belief maintains that people are only valuable if they have distinguishing abilities: for example, to win gold medals at the Olympics or to be a famous musician. To the contrary the Bible says that the Lord *"will rejoice over you with singing"* (Zephaniah 3:17b). We do not need to earn distinction from God. He loves each one of us and we can bring pleasure to Him by our love.

Yet another worldly belief is that people must have the right background or own lots of possessions to be valuable. However, the heart of the Gospel is that every person, regardless of upbringing or status, can stand on level ground at the Cross of Jesus Christ. We are valuable because we *"were bought at a price"* (1 Corinthians 6:20a).

The world's value system is therefore based on lies from the devil: lies which he has spoken into people's minds over and over again, throughout the course of history. Such lies have influenced how we see ourselves, how we behave and how we treat others. Lies have a phenomenal impact. In fact many of us don't realise that their influence may carry over into our Christian lives. Kay was certainly unaware of this as a young Christian.

Speaking recently to a group of young people, Kay shared that as a child she readily believed as truth all the negative things which people said about her. "During my school days, in particular, I remember making a lot of mistakes while learning to use one of the sewing machines. Sometimes my teacher would get impatient and say, 'Can't you do anything right?' And on one occasion when I made a big blunder, one of the other students said, 'You're stupid!' The sting of these negative words went deep into my spirit and after a while I began to believe that they were true.

"When I was at high school an incident happened which reinforced my negative view of myself. One of my teachers, who was quite a cynical lady and a bit of a perfectionist, was asking different members of the class to comment on a passage of Shakespeare. As she began to call on various students I fervently hoped she wouldn't ask me. I found Shakespeare difficult to understand at the best of times, and this wasn't a particularly easy passage. I was asked, however, so I gave the teacher my comments. In response, she laughed! I felt so embarrassed and humiliated, and as the teacher continued to laugh, I committed myself never to give my comments on anything again.

"As a result of this incident, whenever the teacher asked me a question my mind went completely blank, I became tongue tied and felt extremely awkward. Yet as soon as the class was over, I would begin to think of the things I could have said.

"Although I didn't realise it at the time, my negative self-image carried over into my life as a Christian. I remember going to a meeting and being asked for my opinion about a particular issue. After I'd said what I thought, the others disagreed and immediately I felt I must be wrong. I decided that in future I'd keep my opinions to myself and from then on, whenever a discussion arose about an issue, I'd retreat into myself. If anyone asked what I thought, I'd shrug my shoulders and give a non-committal response, believing that if I said what I thought they'd think it stupid and therefore reject me!

"As a result of these experiences and the decisions I had made to withdraw, I despised myself instead of accepting and loving myself as God did. My identity was based on believing the negative words and reactions of others, rather than the truth of God's word. What's more, the inner vow I'd made to *never* give my opinion again enabled Satan to lock me into myself and prevent me from doing the things God asked me to do.

"Freedom started to come when I recognised that by despising myself I'd despised what God had said was good. I began to realise that I'd been listening to lies, instead of the truth which God had spoken. With this realisation I repented of my unbelief and asked God's forgiveness. I also specifically repented from making these inner vows and received God's forgiveness and release from their effects in my life. Then I began reading scriptures in the Bible which spoke about God's love for me and I began thanking Him for the value which I have in His eyes. Now, when negative words are directed to me, instead of receiving them as true, I'm learning to focus on the truth of God's word and know my true identity in Him!"

As Christians we will continually be tempted in these two areas: "Is God who He says He is?" and "Am I who God says I am?" Satan knows only too well that if he can convince us to shift our focus away from the truth of God's word we will rapidly spiral downwards. He tried to convince Jesus; he will try to convince us. We can, however, learn from the way Jesus responded to Satan's taunts. Let's look briefly at one example, noting the sequence of events.

In Luke's gospel account he records that during Jesus' baptism God the Father affirmed His Son, saying, "*You are my son, whom I love; with you I am well pleased*" (Luke 3:22). This was a significant statement. Not only was it a declaration to the world and to Satan, but it was a personal statement to Jesus, concerning His identity.

Immediately after the Father declares Jesus' true identity, however, Satan says to Jesus, "*If* you are the Son of God, then. . . " In other words, "Maybe you're not really who God says you are . . . ?"

The devil then taunts Jesus, tempting Him to confirm His identity by performing miraculous signs. Yet how does Jesus respond? He doesn't waste words or actions justifying who He is, but speaks out the truth of God's Word. We see that Satan cannot withstand the power of such truth and is forced to leave Jesus alone. Jesus knew who He was and acted accordingly.

Likewise, each of us need to know who we are! Not only are we a unique part of God's creation, made in His image and likeness, but now through Christ we have become His sons and daughters.[21] God does not love us because we spend time reading the Bible, praying or doing good works. Although we should do these things, He loves us because we are His children.[22] The unchanging word of God needs to be our basis for truth, rather than our feelings which can change from day to day.

If we stand on the truth of God's word, secure in our identity as His sons and daughters, Satan's taunts will not harm us. However, if we do fail to remain secure when our identity is tested and we slacken our belt, we can repent and then re-commit ourselves to believe and live by the truth of who we are in God.

In any spiritual battle the truth is being contested. *"Stand firm then, with the belt of truth buckled around your waist"* (Ephesians 6:14a). A commitment to truth does not just mean getting rid of evil thoughts, but an active application of truth to our minds and hearts. Let us then commit ourselves to base our lives on truth, and refute the devil's lies by focusing on who God is and who He says we are in Him.

Questions

1. What are some of God's true characteristics?

2. What are some Scriptures which speak about our true value?

3. Has the devil's lies affected our self-image?

4. What must we do to stand on truth rather than listen to the devil's lies?

Chapter 9

Stand in Righteousness

Once our commitment to truth has been established, Paul exhorts us to make sure the *"breastplate of righteousness"* is in place (Ephesians 6:14b). The Roman soldier knew what a vital piece of armour the breastplate was. It protected a very vulnerable area, the heart. If he charged into battle without his breastplate in place, leaving his heart unprotected, one thrust with a sword into this vital organ and he'd be dead.

In a similar way, as Christians our spiritual lives have vulnerable areas that need protection. One very vulnerable area is our heart. In Proverbs 4:23 we read, *"Above all else, guard your heart, for it is the wellspring of life."* In other words, our heart is the motivation centre for all that we do. We therefore need to ask ourselves, "Why are we doing what we're doing?"

If Jesus is the lord of our lives, our heart's motivation for doing anything should be to please Him. Luke 10:27 reads, *"Love the Lord your God with all your heart and with all your soul and with all your strength and with all your mind; and love your neighbour as yourself."* This is what pleases God. The motivation for everything we do should be to love God and love others. Satan, of course, has no heart to please God; nor does he want us to have one. Therefore, he will seek to divert us from loving the Lord with all our heart, mind, soul and strength.

One of the ways in which the devil will tempt us to lower the guard over our heart is through lust. It's significant that the exhortation in Proverbs to guard our hearts comes just before a warning, in the next chapter, against immorality! Let me give you an example.

Tom was having problems with his prayer life and came to me for counsel. After we'd talked for a while he confessed that some time back he'd picked up a few pornographic magazines and looked through them – just out of curiosity! However, Tom's interest was aroused and he began to study the pictures more intently. Before long Tom was buying pornographic magazines when he was tired or away from home and on his own. As time went on he realised that not only was he spending increasing amounts of money on pornographic literature, but what began as a casual interest was now a consuming habit. One of the results of this habit was that Tom's prayer life was affected.

As Tom and I together retraced the sequence of events which had occurred, he realised that his heart motive was wrong. Instead of desiring to please God he wanted to satisfy his curiosity. As Tom looked at the magazines he gave the devil grounds to tempt him further. Once his interest was aroused, it became harder to resist further temptation. The devil was therefore able to successfully divert Tom from loving God with all his mind. In fact, Tom allowed the devil to establish a stronghold in his life by indulging in this heart lust.

Convicted of his sin, Tom repented and asked the Lord for forgiveness. A few weeks later when I saw him I asked how his prayer life was going and was encouraged, not only by his positive verbal response, but also by his appearance. There was a new vitality about him which spoke volumes.

Release for Tom came when he not only realised the root cause of his problem but also took offensive action. Repentance was the turning point. As Tom confessed his sin of lust and repented, his relationship with the Lord was restored. Jesus had defeated the devil through His atoning death on the Cross and Tom had taken hold of this victory for himself by his repentance. Through the Holy Spirit he received afresh the righteousness of Christ. Because of the change in Tom's heart, brought about by the work of the Holy Spirit, he was then able to put up a guard around his heart by choosing not to indulge in pornographic literature. Such offensive action, using the breastplate of righteousness, successfully defeated the devil's strategy to divert Tom from loving the Lord with all his heart.

Yet not only will Satan tempt us to get involved in wrong activities; he also seeks to divert us from loving the Lord with a full heart by doing things which appear to be right, but from the wrong motives!

It's amazing how so many of our activities seem to be the right thing to do. For example, going to a prayer meeting can appear to be right on the surface; but it will not be right if the Lord has been speaking to us about spending more time with our family.

A further example is selecting people for tasks simply based on their ability. For instance, it may seem logical to ask a talented musician to join the worship group at church – or even to lead the worship. While we do need skilled people in such roles, God is far more interested in the motivation of their heart. Are they really there to worship Him, or are they preoccupied with their own instruments and musical abilities? What is their motive?

An area in my own life where I need to check my heart, to see if my motive is righteous, involves discussions. I enjoy a good debate in which ideas are batted to and fro – especially if I'm winning! It's therefore quite natural for me to enjoy discussing the various questions non-Christians ask, such as, "What about the person who has never heard about Jesus; will he go to hell?"

Yet while it's important to have answers to these kind of questions, on occasions I've found myself getting so involved in a debate with someone that the discussion has become quite heated, and I've entered into an argumentative spirit!

At times like that the Holy Spirit has nudged me, saying, "If you win this argument you're going to lose this man." At that point I've needed to stop arguing and make a conscious effort to listen to that person. Then, when things have cooled down and he's realised that I'm interested in him, the opportunity has come for me to speak again. I've then been able to simply give my testimony of how God has changed my life, and in doing so, allow the love of God to flow through me to him.

As a result of such experiences I'm now aware that before witnessing to anyone I need to check my motives, asking myself, "Am I motivated by a love for God, desiring to reach out with His love to others, or am I motivated simply by a selfish ambition to win arguments?"

This question is one which we need to ask ourselves about anything we do. As Jeremiah says, *"The heart is deceitful above all things and beyond cure. Who can understand it?"* (Jeremiah 17:9). We can often be selfishly motivated, having a great need to bring our hearts, as well as our deeds, under the lordship of Christ.

It is for this reason that we need to see the breastplate as a breastplate of *righteousness*. What is righteousness? It involves a right standing with the Lord which can't be achieved through the good things we may do; it is only taken hold of through Christ's atoning death on the Cross. As Paul says in an earlier chapter, *"You were once in darkness, but now you are light in the Lord. Live as children of the light (for the fruit of the light consists in all goodness, righteousness and truth) and find out what pleases the Lord"* (Ephesians 5:8-10).

Through our faith in Christ's atoning death on the Cross we are declared righteous with God. As we learn to walk in righteousness our focus changes from pleasing ourselves to desiring to please God. Maintaining that focus is where the work comes in – and it is work! We need to ensure that our heart is guarded from the attacks of Satan, remembering that his aim is to divert us from loving God with our full heart.

Perhaps as you are reading this chapter the Lord is highlighting difficulties which you have in the vulnerable area of your heart. It may be that you also struggle with lust; or is may be other areas such as selfish ambition, envy, resentment, impatience, dissension, hatred, thoughts of violence . . . If the Holy Spirit is bringing things to mind, why not stop now and confess the specific sin to the Lord, using the following prayer as a guideline:

"Lord Jesus, I realise that I've sinned against You and others through my habit of . . . I repent of . . . and ask you to forgive me. I want You to be truly Lord of my life in this area and I desire to please You by loving You with my heart, mind, soul and strength."

If you've prayed along these lines may I encourage you to follow through with this commitment to the Lord. Paul's motive in speaking about a soldier's armour is initially to make us aware of our vulnerability, and then to draw our attention to the place where we're most likely to be attacked, so we can be on the alert. We then need to apply to our lives the understanding gained.

As we recognise that the motivation of our heart determines our spiritual vitality, it's evident that our heart is therefore a vulnerable area. To protect it we need to ensure that the *"breastplate of righteousness"* is in place, as we regularly allow the Holy Spirit to examine our motives for doing things.

Questions:

1. How can we please God?

2. What does it mean to stand in righteousness?

Chapter 10

Stand Ready

Continuing his analogy between a Roman soldier and a Christian in battle, Paul now focuses on the armour needed for our feet. He exhorts us to have our *"feet fitted with the readiness that comes from the gospel of peace"* (Ephesians 6:15).

The Roman soldier's shoes were also a vital part of his battle gear. Josephus described them as "shoes thickly studded with sharp nails" so as to ensure a good grip. Furthermore, they were "fitted" to his feet. Historical accounts reveal that a soldier would wear his shoes at all times, so that he was always ready for battle.

In contrast to the Roman soldier, quite often when I'm physically tired and want to relax I'll take my shoes off and put my feet up. That's okay. Not so with my spiritual shoes. I don't want to slip off my spiritual readiness to respond to the Holy Spirit's promptings. It's this type of readiness that Paul alludes to here.

My spiritual readiness was tested recently. Kay and I had a very busy week and we were looking forward to a relaxing weekend. A friend of ours had been staying with us for a few days but he would leave on Saturday morning, and we weren't expecting any other visitors.

Our friend missed his plane, however, and asked us both to join him in praying about what to do until he could get a seat on another flight. As we prayed together we all felt prompted to go and see Sue, a girl who we knew was in need. Quite honestly it was the last thing I felt like doing, but we knew the Holy Spirit was prompting us, so we went to visit Sue and spent time praying for her. The result was that the Lord brought a measure of healing to her.

At the end of the day, although we'd spent several hours in prayer, Kay and I felt more refreshed that when the day began. We realised that as we'd responded in obedience to the prompting of the Holy Spirit, He had not only used us as a channel for His healing power, but also refreshed us spiritually *and* physically. This experience also showed us that while our original plans to put our feet up and relax physically were fine, it was just as well we hadn't put our feet up spiritually, as on that particular day the Lord wanted to use us. We needed to be spiritually ready!

Christians are often faced with temptations to yield their spiritual readiness. Let's look at a situation in the Old Testament where someone does just that. *"In the spring, at the time when kings go off to war, David sent Joab out with the king's men and the whole Israelite army. They destroyed the Ammonites and besieged Rabbah. But David remained in Jerusalem. One evening David got up from his bed and walked around on the roof of the palace. From the roof he saw a woman bathing. The woman was very beautiful, and David sent someone to find out about her . . ."* (2 Samuel 11:1-4).

Note that at the time when kings go to war, David remained in Jerusalem. Part of his job description was to go into battle (as is part of our calling). Yet David conveniently ignored what it meant to be king and by remaining in Jerusalem, shirking a major responsibility, he was tempted spiritually.

We then read that "one evening David got up from his bed." (Usually we get up in the morning!) It could be that the warm spring days with nothing to do meant that he spent most of his time relaxing with his feet up, and therefore wasn't tired enough to sleep throughout the night. Or it could be that David was feeling guilty about not being out in the battle, and couldn't sleep. Either way his laziness made him vulnerable to temptation. And as we read further, the story goes on to record a sequence of events: David saw Bathsheba bathing, he wanted to find out about her, had her brought to the palace, and then he committed adultery with her. David had taken his spiritual shoes off!

Once David had yielded his spiritual readiness to Satan he was tempted to sin further, and as a result, murdered Uriah, Bathsheba's husband. We then see evidence of God's mercy as Nathan, the prophet, confronts David with his sin. In response, David acknowledges his guilt and repents of his sin. Through his repentance, David is restored in his relationship with the Lord and Satan's power is broken in this area of his life.

If the devil is to be powerless in our lives as Christians we need to stand ready, not allowing ourselves to be vulnerable to his temptations. One of the ways to maintain readiness is to make sure that we're not being spiritually lazy. But there's a second aspect of readiness which Paul talks about: a readiness to wear the shoes of "the gospel of peace."

Because the gospel can bring peace to those who are at enmity with God, our shoes are not only sturdy, able to ensure sure footing and cover much terrain, but God sees them as beautiful. In Isaiah 52:7 we read,

> *"How beautiful on the mountains*
> *are the feet of those who bring good news,*
> *who proclaim peace,*
> *who bring good tidings,*
> *who proclaim salvation,*
> *who say to Zion, 'Your God reigns!"*

The message of salvation which has brought life, freedom and beauty to our lives is one which can transform others' lives. Paul reminds us of this as he refers to the shoes as those of the gospel of peace – and he does so for a reason.

As we've considered earlier, Satan prowls around the earth looking for those he can devour. His message is not peace but discord; not life but death; not freedom but slavery. He will therefore seek to prevent us from taking the message of peace to those who need to hear it.

Many times those who are most needy are not far away. They are people we rub shoulders with in the factory, office or classroom. If we have our spiritual shoes on we'll be ready to take this message, as the Holy Spirit prompts us, to these people with whom we have daily contact – or with people we might meet on the bus, train or plane.

About a year ago I boarded a plane from America for a long trip back to England. I'd been on a business trip and was exhausted by endless meetings, so I sat down in my seat, looking forward to reading my book and being able to withdraw from others.

Yet after the plane was airborne I began to feel uneasy about not communicating with the woman sitting beside me. This was unusual for me, as I don't normally feel a compulsion to witness to everyone. But in this instance I felt the Holy Spirit was prompting me. So I began to ask her where she was travelling to and in the ensuing conversation I discovered that her husband had died very recently. She was in extreme grief.

This woman was open to hearing about a Man who had not only experienced grief Himself[23] but had borne our griefs and sorrows upon the Cross and could bring healing to her own heart.[24] Thus, over the next few hours I had an opportune time to talk about the "gospel of peace" with this woman, sharing how Jesus could meet her need. Although she didn't commit her life to Him during the flight, the letters which Kay and I have received from her since have encouraged us to believe that the Holy Spirit is continuing to reveal Jesus to her.

To make the most of that situation I had to have my spiritual shoes on, so that I could receive the Holy Spirit's prompting to share the gospel of peace. Because I tend to withdraw from people at times when I'm tired, it's a vulnerable area for me and I'm sure I've missed many opportunities on other occasions.

As we each seek to live our lives for the Lord and work in partnership with Him in the spiritual battle, let's pray for spiritual readiness to respond to the promptings of the Holy Spirit, and a readiness at all times to share the gospel of peace with those in need. In other words, to have our *"feet fitted with the readiness that comes from the gospel of peace"* (Ephesians 6:15).

Questions

1. Why did David lose his spiritual readiness?

2. How can we physically relax and yet still have our spiritual shoes on?

Chapter 11

Stand When Tempted

Each one of us faces temptation in our daily lives. The question is, how do we handle it? We have two choices: to give in to temptation and therefore sin, or to endure temptation. *"Blessed is the man that endureth temptation . . ."* (James 1:13 KJV). God promises blessing if we will stand firm when tempted.

Not only has God given us power to stand on truth, to stand in righteousness and to stand ready, but He has also given us the power to stand when tempted. In other words He has given us the power, through faith in Jesus, to overcome temptation. However, if we are to take a firm stand when tempted, we need to understand what actually happens. Who tempts us and what does temptation involve?

James answers the first question by saying, *"Let no one say when he is tempted, 'I am tempted by God; for God cannot be tempted with evil and He Himself tempts no one"* (James 1:13 RSV). Clearly God is not the author of temptation. That leaves two possibilities: the devil or our own hearts.

Reading further in James's letter, it appears that *both* ourselves and Satan are participants in the temptation process. James says, *"each person is tempted when he is lured and enticed by his own desire. Then desire when it is conceived gives birth to sin; and sin when it is full grown brings forth death"* (James 1:14-15 RSV).

"Conceived" is a helpful image here. Just as it takes two people to "conceive" a baby, two participants are involved in the conception of sin. We make an active choice and Satan applies his pressure to it. How does that happen? Let's consider these two verses more closely.

The first stage in the temptation sequence occurs when we're enticed through our own desire. The word "desire" can apply, for example, to the normal bodily drives which we have for food, sex, and rest etc. These desires in themselves are healthy and good, when used in the ways God intended. For example, eating in moderation, sex within the context of a committed marriage relationship, and sleeping for a reasonable amount of time each night are all desires being properly used. However, the word "enticed" suggests that our desires can become heightened, therefore requiring greater satisfaction than is legitimate. In other words, our senses become over excited. (This is due to the atmosphere of the world in which we live, where much advertising is geared towards gratifying our physical desires.) We then respond to the excitement and are therefore more prone to temptation. At this point we become vulnerable to enticement by the enemy.

To lure and entice is actually a common fishing practice. A fisherman drops some bait to attract the fish; a fish sees the bait and desires it; it responds to the desire by biting the bait and is then caught. Two participants are involved: the fisherman and the fish.

Likewise, the enemy will sometimes attract us to indulge excessively in a natural desire. He does this by heightening the desire, enticing us to indulge in it excessively. For example, he may tempt us to over-indulgence in food (gluttony), sex (immorality, adultery, or other forms of uncleanness) or rest (laziness).

At this point, of course, there is a choice to be made. This is where the second stage of the temptation sequence occurs: how we respond in our hearts. Will we allow the attraction of the bait to influence our emotions beyond what is natural – heightening our desire as David did when he saw Bathsheba? Or will we admit that although the bait is attractive, we will also resist the lure, as Joseph did when Potiphar's wife attempted to seduce him? Note that temptation is not in itself sin. Actively giving in to temptation is where sin takes place.

Our heart's response will determine our actions. This is the third stage of the temptation sequence. We can either "give birth to sin," as David did by looking lustfully at Bathsheba and then committing adultery with her. Or we can run as Joseph did when recognising the intentions of Potiphar's wife and quickly making the decision to flee from the scene.

Why was Joseph successful in overcoming temptation and David was not? I believe the key to Joseph's success was firstly the decision he'd previously made in his heart not to sin against God. This is a profound key for winning the battle against temptation. The reason we often lose the battle is that we've not committed ourselves ahead of time to reject temptation. Hence, when the temptation approaches we are "unstable" (see James 1:8) or wishy-washy. There's no previous determination in us, causing us to fend off the temptation. Yet there was in Joseph for he had obviously set his will to follow God and not to sin. We read his response in Genesis 39:9: *"How then could I do such a wicked thing and sin against God?"*

Joseph had not put himself in the place of

temptation, whereas David was idle and living in disobedience, prone to temptation. Sin, when not dealt with, leads to further sin. This is evident in David's life as he not only commits adultery with Bathsheba, but then also murders her husband.[25] Joseph's heart response indicates that he was doing his normal job and living in right relationship to the Lord. He wasn't looking for something to fill a void in his life, therefore he was in a better position to flee temptation.

Similarly, it will be easier for us to resist temptation in our lives if we stand by our inner decision not to sin, daily committing our lives to the lordship of Christ. But we also need to reinforce this commitment by making sure that we're not putting ourselves in situations where we will be vulnerable to temptation. This is particularly necessary in areas where we've sinned in the past. The enemy knows our areas of weakness and will try to entice us again. We need to take practical steps to avoid putting ourselves in a position where his bait will attempt to lure us.

For example, if we've been involved in sexual sin we need to guard our thought life and emotions from being stimulated in this way. Steve was one person who found this out the hard way.

Steve and Lisa were part of the same church that we attended several years ago. Kay and I had got to know them fairly well and we sometimes prayed together. They were young Christians and Steve had been sexually involved in other relationships before he got married. Steve had a job on a building site. He was usually very tired at the end of the day, and one of the ways in which he liked to relax was to watch television in the evening.

As time went on Steve found himself watching

more television programmes than he'd intended and staying up later in the evening. Steve was not only relaxing physically, he was relaxing spiritually. He started to become lethargic and spiritually passive. His ability to discern between what was okay to watch and what was not suitable was weakened. Soon Steve was watching programmes which were sexually provocative, and as a consequence, his thoughts and emotions were affected.

Although realising he was getting into problems, Steve was nonetheless attracted by the content of the programmes he was watching. When Lisa began to question him about the amount of time he spent in front of the television, Steve consistently justified his actions. His usual response was, "Honey, you know I need to unwind – and the television helps me to do that. I'm not doing anything wrong."

After some time, however, Steve became so dissatisfied with the state of his thought life that he came to me for counsel. Although I identified his problems to be caused by the excessive amount of time he was watching television, it took a while before he was willing to admit that this was the case.

Once Steve recognised the source of his temptations, and his apathetic response, he repented from his sin of sensuality. He received God's forgiveness and cleansing of his mind and heart. Then he asked Lisa and me to keep a check on the amount of time that he spent watching television, and what type of programme he was viewing. Being accountable for his actions and his thought life reinforced Steve's inner commitment to make Jesus lord of his desires.

Areas where we've sinned in the past will be particular targets for the enemy. It could be indulging a desire excessively, such as money, sex, power, food, rest. Or it may be giving into other forms of sin, such as pride, unforgiveness, criticism. therefore it's vital that we not only make an inner commitment to righteousness but that we also reinforce our stand by avoiding situations where we could be tempted.

However, if we are tempted, there is a way out! Just as being tempted involves a process, there's also a process for overcoming temptation.

Firstly, we need to recognise the *source* of the temptation: our heightened desire, the devil, or a combination of both. God is not the author of temptation. Let's remember that.

Secondly, we need to resist the lure of the bait, although it may be attractive. Or, as someone has said, "We can't stop the birds from flying over our head but we can stop them building a nest in our hair." Similarly, there can be a stream of thoughts flowing through our minds, clamouring for attention and without invitation. But while we can't always control what comes into our mind we can control what stays there. We can say, "No" to the mental temptations.[26]

Thirdly, we need to do some rethinking; looking for things which we can say, "Yes" to. As it says in Philippians 4:8, "*whatever is true . . . noble . . . right . . . pure . . . lovely . . . admirable . . . think on these things.*" I've found that recalling verses of scripture, which I've previously memorised, is a helpful way to turn my mind away from tempting thoughts.

Once we've come to this point, we can ask the Holy Spirit to fill us afresh with His grace and power to stand firm. In chapter seven we considered what it meant to "*be filled with the Spirit*" (Ephesians 5:18). The Greek translation of this verse refers not to one infilling but regular infilling! We are to keep "being" filled so that we're constantly receiving God's strength and power to stand firm in our daily lives. If we attempt to stand on our own we'll find ourselves in a treadmill, trying to overcome . . . trying to overcome . . .! However, if we receive God's power to stand, we will be able to endure. We will be able to stand firm when tempted.

Questions:

1. How can we prepare ourselves to handle temptation when it comes?

2. Is there an area in your life where you are likely to be tempted? If so, what action should you take so that you will stand firm?

Chapter 12

Stand in Faith

"In addition to all this," Paul says to the Ephesian church, *"take up the shield of faith, with which you can extinguish the flaming arrows of the evil one"* (Ephesians 6:16). Paul realised that faith in God was crucial if Christians were to keep standing firm in the midst of the devil's attacks.

Comparing faith to a soldier's shield, Paul was highlighting the defensive aspect of faith in the spiritual battle. Primarily the Roman soldier used his shield to protect himself against the enemy, yet he didn't cower behind his shield in fear. He held it purposefully in front of him to deflect the enemy's missiles and to enable him to stand firm in the battle.

Likewise, Paul not only urges Christian soldiers to take up their spiritual shields, but to raise them confidently, expressing faith in the all-powerful God to triumph over the devil's attacks.

This exhortation to stand in faith is not made lightly. Paul was confident in faith's foundations. These foundations could be summed up as firstly, God's character, which is unchanging. Secondly, His written Word, the Bible. Thirdly, His Word of authority, spoken by the Holy Spirit. Such truths are unshakeable and provide the basis for standing in faith in God to resist the devil.

Note that Paul does not minimize the nature of the devil's opposition. He is realistic about the *"flaming arrows of the evil one,"* knowing only too well what is was like to have temptations hurled at him, or to be in difficult situations. Nevertheless, he also knows that God's power is greater that any obstacle. He therefore urges Christians to find ways to express their faith in God, in the midst of their difficulties.

Several years ago I remember struggling with a difficult problem, and not finding any way out of it. After some days had passed the Lord began to show me that my prayers were very negative. In fact, looking back now I'd call them "lament sessions," as my prayer would be along these lines: "Lord, this problem is really getting me down. I just can't see any way out of it. Why does this always happen to me . . .? Please help me."

Such a prayer is really a negative lament. Yet the Bible quite strongly says that *"without faith it's impossible to please God"* (Hebrews 11:6). I needed to realise that if I wasn't praying in faith, I wasn't acknowledging anything. Instead of fixing my eyes on God, who is all powerful, I was focusing on the problem which only made the situation worse.

The following story highlights the issue further. Two children were getting ready for bed. As they were snuggling down underneath the blankets little Johnny piped up that he was scared of ghosts. Wanting to help her young brother, Linda began to pray: "Dear Lord, please don't let there be footsteps across the ceiling tonight." She paused, and then continued fervently saying, "And Lord, please don't let there be chains rattling in the cupboard." Then, praying even more earnestly, she pleaded, "And Lord, please don't let there be screams from under the bed!"

By the end of his sister's prayer poor Johnny was more scared than he'd ever been. His mind was now firmly fixed upon his problem: fear of ghosts. In a similar way, when you or I struggle with a difficult situation or a "flaming arrow" from the evil one, if we focus on the problem instead of focusing on the Lord, it's possible to feel worse after praying that if we'd never prayed at all. When we pray we need to take the problem to the Lord and leave it with Him, trusting Him for the solution.

Expressing faith in God while in the midst of a difficult situation acts as a defensive shield against the devil's attacks, enabling us to stand firm and know the deliverance of the Lord.

Recently, one of the families on our YWAM base experienced what it was like to stand in faith in the face of a seemingly impossible situation. Stuart and Barbara, a middle-aged couple, had been on the staff with YWAM for five and a half years. As they were praying together over the Christmas period, the Lord began to show them that it was time to return home and take on a salaried job. Both of them agreed that this was the word of the Lord for them; but there were two major problems. They had no home nor any prospect of a job! To the natural eye the situation looked impossible to solve, yet Stuart and Barbara resolved to ask God for His solution.

Initially they prayed as a couple, bringing the problem to the Lord and affirming their trust in Him to work things out for good. Then later on, as Stuart and Barbara prayed further with some friends, one person felt prompted to read 2 Chronicles 20:17, inserting their names in the verse so that it read, *"You will not have to fight this battle. Take up your positions; stand firm and see the deliverance the Lord will give you, O Stuart and Barbara. Do not be afraid; do not be discouraged."*

Hearing this scripture read out, Stuart and Barbara

immediately knew that it was God's answer to their problem. It was as though the verse leapt within both of them at the same time. During the next couple of months as they recalled these words, they kept affirming their trust in God's promise to them.

There were times, however, when Barbara started to look at the natural circumstances. They were holding onto the Lord's promise but nothing seemed to be happening. At such times the impossibility of the situation began to fill her thoughts. (This was exactly what her unseen enemy wanted: to see Barbara get frustrated and waver in her faith.) Yet in the midst of her frustration the words, *"Do not be discouraged"* kept coming back into her mind. At that point Barbara would lift up her shield of faith, saying, "Lord, You said we wouldn't have to fight this battle. I put my trust in what You've spoken." (This declaration of faith in God's faithfulness silenced the voice of the enemy.) She would then begin to worship the Lord, focusing on the truth of His character. As she did so, her faith was rekindled.

Barbara's faith in God's promise grew considerably in the following weeks when the Lord miraculously provided the solution to one of their needs. Stuart heard about a vacancy in the firm where he'd previously worked and made an enquiry by telephone. Although he knew many of the staff, the employers had changed since Stuart had left. He was therefore unprepared for the question, "When can you start?" He was offered the job without having an interview! ("You will not have to fight this battle," said the Lord.)

Rejoicing in the Lord's provision of a job, Stuart and Barbara began looking for a house. Finding the prices to be much higher than they'd anticipated, they were even more aware that they could do nothing to meet their need. Returning to the base they prayed, "Lord, we need a miracle; there's nothing we can do apart from standing firm and trusting You. Thank You that You've said we don't need to fight this battle. We stand on the truth of who You are and what You've said."

A few days after Stuart and Barbara prayed in this way a man whom they'd met only a few times telephoned them. He'd felt prompted by the Lord to help them with their housing need. This "help" turned out to be a very substantial gift, enabling Stuart and Barbara to take out a mortgage on a house. God had truly fought the battle for them, providing both the job and the money that they needed! Their part was to stand firm holding up their shields of faith by taking their concerns to the Lord and trusting in Him to bring about His solution.

Likewise, God is able to confound the unseen enemy in each of the battles you and I face – whether it's a financial battle, a difficult situation at work, or an area of struggle in a relationship. Instead of lamenting over the problem, God's plan is that we "take up the shield of faith," focusing on Him in the midst of the difficulty, and stand firm.

Questions

1. What are the foundations of faith?

2. How can we exercise faith in a powerful God in the midst of a difficult situation?

SECTION THREE:
"LET'S FIGHT"

Chapter 13

Fight With Faith and Hope

In the previous chapters the focus has been on the defensive aspects of spiritual warfare, i.e. standing against the devil's attacks. Now it's time to consider the offensive side to the battle, i.e. fighting the adversary.

When Jesus said to His disciples, *"I will build my church and the gates of Hades will not overcome it,"* He was not speaking about fortifying church buildings but about mobilising the people of God. His intention was, and still is, that His people spiritually move forward in the battle, penetrating the gates of hell.

These gates will not be knocked down with laser beams, tanks or bombs. They will, however, yield to spiritual weapons. Two powerful weapons are faith and hope in God.

The book of Acts records that after the early disciples were filled with the Holy Spirit they began exercising faith and hope in Jesus the risen Lord. They saw people freed from captivity, sinners received forgiveness and the sick were healed. Oppressed people were released into joy. The devil's strongholds were routed by the power of God.

Yet such experiences were not intended for the early disciples alone. Throughout church history God has been calling His people to firstly stand in the battle and then, through faith and hope in His power, to take offensive action against the devil's works. A Biblical example of a young man who responded to this call and then engaged in the battle was David, the shepherd.

The story of David and Goliath is familiar to most Sunday School children, yet it's more than a good story. David's responses in the midst of the situation confronting him, clearly illustrate his godly perspective of the battle and provide an example for Christians to follow.

Arriving at the Israelite camp, David found his brothers and the rest of the army paralysed with fear in the face of Goliath, the Philistine giant. The name Goliath means, *"an exile or soothsayer."* (The Philistines were involved in the occult as soothsayers – see Isaiah 2:6.)

Goliath was *"over nine feet tall. He had a bronze helmet on his head and wore a coat of scale armour of bronze weighing five thousand shekels; on his legs he wore bronze greaves, and a bronze javelin was slung on his back"* (1 Samuel 17:4b-6). Confronted by such a formidable opponent, the Israelites felt completely powerless. When David walked into the camp he found the whole army lamenting about this terrible situation.

After seeing Goliath himself and hearing his defiant taunts, David's response was not to focus on the problem but to fix his gaze upon his all-powerful God. *"Who is this uncircumcised Philistine that he should defy the armies of the living God?"* (1 Samuel 17:26b). Note that he does not call the Israelites the armies of Saul, but the armies of the living God. When the Israelites compared Saul with Goliath they were terrified. By comparing Goliath with God, David had the true perspective.

Having proclaimed his trust in the Lord, David volunteered to go out and fight Goliath. Saul agreed to let him try and proceeded to dress him in his own armour. David found himself unable to move freely so he took the armour off and went forth trusting in his spiritual weapons of faith and hope in God.

Speaking to the Philistines David declared, "*You come against me with sword and spear and javelin, but I come against you in the name of the Lord Almighty, the God of the armies of Israel, whom you have defied . . . All those gathered here will know that it is not by sword or spear that the Lord saves; for the battle is the Lord's, and he will give all of you into our hands*" (1 Samuel 17:45,47). Then, using a sling and a stone and trusting in the Lord's power, David struck Goliath down.

Similarly, you and I can see the spiritual giants in our lives defeated as we gain a true perspective on the situation before us (remember how Elijah prayed that his servant would be given spiritual eyes to see) and then exercise faith and hope in God.

In order to move forward in the spiritual battle, taking offensive action against the devil's works, faith and hope need to be linked together. Hebrews 11:1 (RSV) reads, "*Now faith is the assurance of things hoped for, the conviction of things not seen.*" In other words, faith is the means by which we obtain the things we're expecting. Because David's faith in God was founded upon the knowledge of His character and His Word, he confidently expected God to move powerfully against the Philistines. Faith *and* hope in God enabled David to stand firm and to take action.

Yet hope is a neglected spiritual weapon for the modern Christian. Generally the word is viewed as having no firm foundation. If anything, "hope" is used in a negative way in many conversations. For example, if I say to Kay, "I hope the children remembered to put out the milk bottles tonight," there's an element of uncertainty in my mind.

Likewise, as Christians we can speak about having hope in God, and yet deep down have many doubts. The devil attempts to magnify these doubts through his various schemes (anxiety, discouragement, confusion and so on) so that confidence in God's character and His Word is diminished.

It's when these thoughts arise that you and I need to submit them to Jesus and apply the victory which He has won – taking *"captive every thought to make it obedient to Christ"* (2 Corinthians 10:5). The result is true Biblically based hope.

I recall a time when my hope in God was tested. As a family we were planning a trip from England to our home country of New Zealand, to spend Christmas with relatives and friends whom we hadn't seen for several years. Just before we began making the necessary travel arrangements I received an invitation to speak at a youth camp in South Africa. The camp would conclude a few days before Christmas. As Kay and I prayed about this invitation we both felt that the Lord was saying I should accept it. It would mean Kay and the children flying to New Zealand before me. I'd join them after the youth camp in South Africa.

The practical difficulties began as I tried to arrange a flight from South Africa to New Zealand. Getting to South Africa was no problem but the travel agent told me that only one flight per week went from South Africa to New Zealand. Not only that, as it was the Christmas period there was a waiting list of two hundred people. The travel agent told me to "Forget it!"

In the face of this seemingly hopeless situation I had a choice to make. Was I going to get anxious and allow the enemy to choke my confidence in God? Or was I going to put my hope in Him, trusting in His ability to work for good in the situation?

At that time I remember reading Hebrews 10:23 (RSV), *"Let us hold fast the confession of our hope without wavering, for he who promised is faithful."* So I committed the problem to the Lord and every day began to speak out my confidence that although this situation looked impossible, He was able to use His resources to make it possible.

Several times during the next few weeks I telephoned our travel agent to check on developments. In addition, I kept in contact with my friends in South Africa who were also trying to get me a seat on the plane. There was no change. It was at these times that negative thoughts came into my mind, as though the devil was saying "It's impossible. You're not going to get on the plane. You won't be able to be with your family for Christmas . . ." Once again the temptation was to get anxious and give up. Yet just at the crucial time I'd remember a Biblical story which would encourage me. I recalled the story of Abraham, who at one hundred years of age grappled with God's word to him that he'd have a son! Yet he didn't allow doubt and unbelief to take hold of his mind. We read that, *"Against all hope, Abraham in hope believed"* (Romans 5:18). Then the scripture goes on to say, *"he grew strong in his faith **as** he gave glory to God, fully convinced that God was able to do what he had promised"* (Romans 5:20b-21 RSV). Abraham put his confidence in God's word.

Along with this story I was further encouraged by

remembering Jeremiah's response when faced with the siege of Jerusalem. He cried out, *"Ah, Sovereign Lord, You have made the heavens and the earth by your great power and outstretched arm. Nothing is too hard for You"* (Jeremiah 32:17). It was as though I heard Jeremiah challenge me, "Barry, is your situation too hard for the Lord?"

As I recalled these testimonies of men who put their confidence in God and saw him fulfill His promises, fresh hope filled me. And hope brought faith, as the Holy Spirit gave me the assurance that in this situation God was working for my good.

A few days later I received a telephone call from my friends in South Africa to say that another flight had been scheduled for the busy Christmas period – something the travel agent had previously said would not happen – and a seat was reserved for me! So, praise the Lord, I could join my family for Christmas. (Let me just add here that when I reached South Africa I found that other Christians were also praying for seats to be released; so it was our combined faith and confidence in God which released His power into the situation.)

The humorous side of this incident occurred when I telephoned our local travel agent, who wasn't a Christian. When I told him that I had a seat on a flight, he said, "That's impossible!" So I gave him the flight details and asked him to check his computer. He did so and was utterly amazed, asking, "How do you people do it?" I remember my reply was, "It's not what you know; it's Who you know!"

The source of our hope is God Himself. As the writer to the Hebrews says, *"We have this hope as an anchor for the soul, firm and secure"* (Hebrews 6:19). Both faith and hope have firm foundations. With faith and hope in the all-powerful God, Christians can stand firm in the battle, not conceding an inch to the devil. Furthermore, we can begin to push back the "gates of Hades" taking territory from him in the spiritual battle.

Questions:

1. How can we fight offensively in the spiritual battle?

2. Why should we be able to fight with confidence?

Chapter 14

Fight With Declaration

Faith and hope in God mobilises Christians to begin pushing back the gates of hell. The momentum is kept going by declaring truth and creating life in the spiritual realm.

From the beginning of time when God spoke those authoritative words, "Let there be . . .," the results were dynamic! Light was separated from darkness at the sound of His voice. Land and sea were divided by His word. Then at His command all living forms came into existence. Genesis chapter one records the incredible results of the declared word of God.

Yet Genesis one was just the beginning. God has continued to speak: through creation itself,[27] through the prophets in the Bible, through His Son, and through the Holy Spirit. He has declared His purposes in the past and continues to speak them forth in the present.

Just as God uses the spoken word to create life, He calls the church to declare His truth, His character and His wonders – knowing that the declarations of His people will also have powerful consequences.

As it's written in Proverbs 18:21, *"The tongue has the power of life and death, and those who love it will eat its fruit."* The devil himself knows this to be true. That's why he seeks to promote words of criticism, unbelief, discouragement, and so on. Such words are instruments of spiritual, and emotional death. Conversely, words of testimony and songs sung in praise to God create life. The tongue can be a source of life and power against the unseen enemy. For this reason Paul exhorts the church to take up the *"sword of the Spirit, which is the Word of God"* (Ephesians 6:17b), and declare words of life.

In this verse, "Word" is translated from "rhema" in the Greek, which means the "spoken word of God." The sword of the Spirit could therefore be defined as the "written word spoken out." In other words, it involves declaring specific truths from the Bible. Note, the spiritual forces of darkness won't be affected simply by waving the Bible at them. Appropriate words of scripture, as led by the Holy Spirit, need to be verbally declared in order to be an effective weapon in the battle.

Declaring scriptural truths doesn't just mean speaking out positive statements. Some people get into trouble by taking hold of a positive thought and concentrating only on that, as though thoughts and words have power in themselves to change situations. Whereas declaration of truth involves responding to the leading of the Holy Spirit and working together in partnership with Him.

Selwyn Hughes tells a story about a woman who described herself as a "positive thinker." Every day for years she would repeat to herself the sentence: "I can deal with every problem that comes my way; nothing can defeat me or overcome me." Then her mother died and, as she put it, "Reality closed in and I went to pieces."

This lady had got so caught up with focusing on "I can do all things," that she'd forgotten the scriptural context, which is *"I can do everything **through Him** who gives me strength"* (Philippians

4:13). Having lost sight of the Lord, she was relying on her own resources, unable to receive and take hold of His strength.

While positive thinking can have the effect of giving a boost in the short term to a person, it will not necessarily change their circumstances. Yet when Christians are led by the Holy Spirit to declare Biblical truth into a situation, He reinforces His Word and circumstances are affected.

Evidence of such a partnership can be seen during Jesus' confrontation with the devil in the wilderness. The Gospel account in Matthew chapter four records that Jesus, full of the Holy Spirit, responded to each temptation with, "It is written," and then spoke out the appropriate scripture. For example, when challenged by the devil about His identity He quoted from Deuteronomy, saying, *"It is written: Man does not live on bread alone, but on every word that comes from the mouth of God"* (Deuteronomy 8:3b). The written word of God spoken out had such authority that the devil's challenges were silenced each time.

You and I can have that same authority in the spiritual battle, as we seek to push back the devil's works of darkness in the power of the Holy Spirit. To exercise that authority we need to understand the power of the spoken word and then apply that understanding, as led by the Holy Spirit.

Paul exhorts Christians to recognise the power of the spoken word in the book of Romans, where he says, *"if you confess with your mouth, 'Jesus is Lord,' and believe in your heart that God raised Him from the dead, you will be saved. For it is with your heart that you believe and are justified, and it is with your mouth that you confess and are saved"* (Romans 10:9-10).

I've prayed with young people who have responded to the Gospel message but sometimes they've had difficulty receiving the assurance of salvation. I remember a young man, called Philip, who came into a Christian coffee bar where I was working. We talked together about the Lord and after a while Philip indicated that he'd like to receive Christ as his Saviour. So I took him into a counselling room, whereupon Philip repented of his sin and then asked Jesus to be His Lord and Saviour.

Philip had been rather glum faced when he'd initially walked into the coffee bar, yet after he'd prayed he didn't look any different.

I remember asking him, "Philip, do you feel any different?" "No," was the morose reply. So I explained to him the importance of believing the facts of salvation and not just his feelings. I also knew that something else needed to take place. Then I had an idea.

Standing up, I beckoned to Philip saying, "come out and meet a friend of mine." As we went into the main part of the coffee bar I said to the leader, "Philip has something to tell you." (Notice what I said – or rather what I did *not* say. I could have said, "Philip has asked Jesus into his heart." But he needed to confess with his own lips.)

Philip was embarrassed and found it difficult to know what to say. But eventually he got it out: "Um . . . I've asked Jesus to be Lord of my life."

Immediately Philip declared those words his countenance changed. The Spirit bore witness with his spirit that he was a child of God and his whole face lit up with the joy of his salvation.

It was the declaration of his own lips that released the Spirit within him. Philip's spoken words also declared to the unseen world that he was turning his back on his old life. He was no longer going to submit to the devil's influence, as Jesus was now his Lord.

Yet the call to "confess with your mouth" doesn't

only apply to our initial conversion experience. Salvation from sin is an ongoing work.[28] You and I are being saved as we continue to believe in our hearts *and* speak out of our mouths the truth about who God is and what He has done.

One of the ways to keep declaring truth is by memorising appropriate verses of scripture. As this becomes a habit, the easier it will be to recall the truth and then speak it as a sword thrust against the enemy, particularly when trying to overcome areas of weakness.

For example, much of my early Christian life was dominated by fear: fear of people, fear of failure, fear of embarrassment by my failures and in particular, fear of speaking in public.

The thought of standing up in front of a group of people and having to say something used to fill me with dread.

Although other Christians prayed with me, and as a result I experienced a measure of freedom, I discovered that God hadn't waved a magic wand over me! I needed to be transformed by the renewal of my mind (see Romans 12:1-2).

My mind began to be renewed as I filled it with God's truth. As well as trying to memorise a new verse of scripture every couple of weeks, I meditated on the verses and then prayed them out as declarations of faith. For example, I'd pray "Thank You Lord that although without You I can do nothing, as I abide in You I can bear much fruit" (see John 15:5). When I filled my mind with God's Word and declared His truth, God released me from the fear which had been a dominating force in my life. Also, when I encountered situations where I'd been tempted to fear, I was able to recall the appropriate scriptures and declare the words of truth to my unseen enemy.

Another form of declaring truth, which effectively

overcomes the enemy, is through words of testimony. In the Psalms David repeatedly exhorts Christians to testify to the Lord's goodness. For example, he cries out, *"Let the redeemed of the Lord say so, whom He has redeemed from the hand of the enemy"* (Psalm 107:2 KJV). When we've experienced the Lord's salvation in our lives we need to speak it out.

David had known God's intervention in times of difficulty, times of discouragement, disappointment or stress. He also knew that remembering these past acts was an important part of further deliverance, both for himself and for his people. As David chose to recall the good things God had done, and verbalised them amidst present struggles, his declaration delivered him from the hand of the enemy. It also opened the way for God to strengthen his faith once more, enabling him to move forward in the spiritual battle.

Christians today need to follow David's example and develop the daily habit of declaring words of testimony. As you and I speak about the Lord's goodness, not only is He exalted and we ourselves are encouraged, but we are less prone to the devil's attacks. Why? Because the enemy is the father of lies and therefore can't stand to be around truth being spoken out. This was certainly true for Maureen some years ago.

A friend and I had stopped to have a cup of tea with Maureen on the way to a meeting. After we'd spent some time talking together, Maureen told us that three days earlier she'd developed a migraine headache which had got worse as time went on. She asked us to pray for her and we readily agreed to do so.

Just as I was about to pray out loud, however, I felt the Holy Spirit restrain me. Instead I was prompted to ask, "Maureen, Who lives in you?" She said, "Jesus, of course." Then I asked, "What has

He done for you?" She replied, "Well, He died on the Cross for my sins." Again I asked, "What else has He done?" she continued to declare her testimony of God's grace to her for about ten minutes. Then, in surprise, she said, "My headache has gone!" We didn't even have to pray.

While I don't believe that every headache is caused by the devil, I think that in Maureen's case it was. And it was the spoken word of her testimony that lifted the oppression. As she started declaring the truth of who Jesus is and what He'd done for her personally, the devil had to flee. He couldn't remain in the presence of truth.

In my own life and in the lives of those I work with, I know that the declaration of our testimony is a powerful thrust against the enemy if we're feeling depressed, discouraged of worthless. It not only overcomes the devil's attacks but also rekindles faith in God, so that we can move forward on confidence, pushing back the devil's lies.

So let us take up the "sword of the Spirit," declaring the truth of who He is and what He has done, to the powers and principalities in the unseen realm. Through our speech let us create words of life which will smash down the gates of hell.

Questions:

1. What is the difference between positive confession and declaring the truth of God's Word?

2. How does the word of our testimony silence the enemy?

3. How can declarations of truth push back the gates of hell?

Chapter 15

Fight With Thanksgiving and Praise

Hand in hand with the sword of the Spirit is the accompanying weapon of thanksgiving and praise. As David proclaims in the Psalms, *"May the praise of God be in their mouths and a double-edged sword in their hands"* (Psalm 149:6). In the Bible praise is offered as soldiers go into battle. As they lift up the name of the Lord, expressing faith and confidence in His character, their focus changes from the present difficulty to God Himself. God responds to faith and releases His Spirit into the situation in power.

Yet many Christians are unaware of the effect of praise in the spiritual realm. While corporate praise times are usually enjoyable – especially if the songs are rousing, the musicians skillful, the worship leader inspiring, and we're doing well spiritually – what happens if one or more of these elements are missing? At such times we often allow our feelings or circumstances to determine whether or not we'll praise the Lord.

For example, sometimes after a long day when I've been busy with meetings, the thought of another meeting makes me feel tired and lethargic. My inner response can then be, "I just don't feel like worshipping tonight." Once again, that is just how our unseen enemy, the devil, wants us to respond.

Yet as Nehemiah proclaimed to his people, *"The joy of the Lord is your strength"* (Nehemiah 8:10b). This joy is not dependent upon circumstances or feelings; it's the result of a relationship with God. Real joy survives amidst the most adverse circumstances, and it is kept alive through thanksgiving and praise to God.

Early on in the Old Testament God stressed the importance of thanksgiving, not only to the children of Israel but also to future generations. Joshua was charged to speak these words to the Israelites: *"Go over before the ark of the Lord your God into the middle of the Jordan. Each of you is to take up a stone on his shoulder, according to the number of the tribes of the Israelites, to serve as a sign among you. In the future, when your children ask you, 'What do these stones mean?' tell them that the flow of the Jordan was cut off before the ark of the covenant of the Lord. When it crossed the Jordan, the waters of the Jordan were cut off. These stones are to be a memorial to the people of Israel forever"* (Joshua 4:5-7).

God's people in the 21st Century also need to establish memorial stones in their lives, to inspire continued gratefulness as well as an expectancy to see Him move in power once more. Recalling times where God brought about past deliverance, extended His forgiveness, or gave grace to endure, inspires further confidence and trust in Him in present and future battles. As thanksgiving and praise become part of our daily walk as Christians, the devil will have a hard job to undermine trust in God, even when times get tough.

Thanksgiving and praise was obviously a habit for Paul and Silas, illustrated by the following account which begins with the response to their preaching in Philippi: *"The crowd joined in the attack against Paul and Silas, and the magistrates ordered them to be stripped and beaten. After they had been severely flogged, they were thrown into prison, and the jailer was commanded to guard them carefully. Upon receiving such orders, he put them in the inner cell and fastened their feet in the stocks. About midnight Paul and Silas were praying and singing hymns to God, and the other prisoners were listening to them"* (Acts 16:22-5).

Imagine the situation! Put yourself in Paul or Silas's position. How would you feel if you'd just been stripped, beaten bloody, and then pinned down into the stocks? Would you naturally feel like starting a worship service? Remember that they were suffering physically, it was the middle of the night, there were no lights and the cell was probably damp and miserable. Not the most encouraging surroundings for worshipping the Lord! Yet here were two men praising God in spite of their conditions. They were giving thanks to God for who He is and for the life He'd given them. This life could not be imprisoned!

Their praises could not be imprisoned either. Their hymns were not sung in an empty void. The records state that "the other prisoners were listening to them." (How could they help it?) Probably they were incredulous at what was going on, wondering, "Who *are* these religious fanatics?"

Not only did Paul and Silas's praises raise their own faith in God but they also acted as a testimony to others. Their testimony was confirmed further by the events which followed. *"Suddenly there was such a violent earthquake that the foundations of the prison were shaken. At once all the prison doors flew open, and everybody's chains came loose"* (Acts 16:26).

The unbelieving might say "It was just a coincidence," yet when earthquakes occur, buildings usually fall on top of people. In this situation, however, all the doors flew open and all the prisoners were freed. They were able to leave the prison unharmed. A miracle happened. God rescued His people.

At this point it's important to clarify that God does not always move in such dramatic ways just because we praise Him. We can't manipulate God to get Him to work for us in a certain way. However, faith in God expressed in praise opens up the channels to receive God's grace. Instead of releasing Paul and Silas from prison God could have given them the grace to endure (as He did for James, who suffered while in prison). Praise is an expression of faith in God when in the midst of overwhelming circumstances. Praise lifts our eyes up to the Lord, enabling us to receive His strength and grace in the situation.

Praise also exalts the Lord in the midst of godlessness. The Lord is *"enthroned on the praises of Israel"* (Psalm 22:3b RSV). Public proclamation of the truth about God affects the spiritual atmosphere. As light and truth penetrate the darkness the devil's influence upon people's lives is diminished.

Some years ago a situation arose with one of the teams in our mission. The team was involved in a weekly evangelistic outreach to a local city. They prayed regularly for the outreach and spent much time endeavouring to talk with people in the city streets but there was very little response. Passers-by were intent on getting their shopping done as quickly as possible, while groups of young people were interested only in the pinball machines situated in the arcades.

After some weeks the team assessed the situation and prayed again. They concluded that the unresponsiveness was not due only to busyness or other interests. There seemed to be an oppression over that part of the city which was hindering their communication.

With this understanding the team leaders decided to stop the evangelism for the time being and to hold praise marches through some of the city streets instead. The purpose of these marches was to enthrone Jesus as Lord over an area of the city by declaring the truth of His word and character to the powers of darkness.

For six weeks the team members gathered together at the normal outreach time and after a time of prayer began walking through the streets openly worshipping the Lord and praising His Name. At the end of that time the difference in the atmosphere was marked. Instead of the feeling of oppression there was a lightness, and whereas previous attempts to share the Gospel had been fruitless, there was now a greater openness to hear and respond. Along with Paul and Silas the evangelism team discovered that declaring the truth about God in the midst of an oppressive situation had an effect upon the unseen spiritual realm.

Satan, of course, knows the benefits of praise and therefore will try to hinder Christians doing so at all costs. His most successful strategy is to try and influence their emotions and thoughts. If he can get people to focus on how they are feeling, and respond accordingly, they'll be vulnerable to depression, self-pity, anxiety and so on. By focusing on our difficulties and feelings we become very inward looking. It is then very difficult to look upwards to the Lord. Similarly, by looking only at the outward circumstances, without attempting to see through the enemy's schemes, it's easy to be disheartened and be tempted to give up. Either way the upward focus towards the Lord is lost, and with it, our ability to work with Him in partnership to fight the unseen enemy.

If we as Christians are to keep our focus on the Lord and receive His grace, understanding and empowering for battle, I believe we need to recognise the importance of thanksgiving and praise in our daily lives. It's essential for our own spiritual well-being. It goes hand in hand with the sword of the Spirit when fighting in the spiritual battle.

Questions

1. What is the basis of our joy as Christians?

2. What are some "memorial stones" for thanksgiving in your life?

3. How does thanksgiving & praise affect the spiritual battle?

Chapter 16

Fight in His Authority

Thanksgiving and praise, declaration of truth, faith and hope in God act as spiritual weapons for Christians to plunder the devil's strongholds. Yet learning to exercise these weapons is futile unless you and I remember that the basis of victory is submission to Jesus. An army only functions effectively if the soldiers are in submission to authority.

Roman soldiers knew what it meant to be under authority. As the centurion who came to Jesus said, *"Just say the word, and my servant will be healed. For I myself am a man under authority, with soldiers under me. I tell this one, 'Go,' and he goes; and that one, 'Come,' and he comes. I say to my servant, 'Do this,' and he does it"* (Matthew 8:8-9). Likewise, Christian soldiers will only be able to exercise authority in the spiritual battle as their lives continue to be under the authority of Jesus.

The danger of trying to use spiritual weapons without being under the authority of Jesus is seen in the following passage: *"Some Jews who went around driving out evil spirits tried to invoke the name of the Lord Jesus over those who were demon possessed. They would say, 'In the name of Jesus, whom Paul preaches, I command you to come out.' Seven sons of Sceva, a Jewish chief priest, were doing this. One day the evil spirit answered them, 'Jesus I know, and I know about*

Paul, but who are you? Then the man who had the evil spirit jumped on them and overpowered them all. He gave them such a beating that they ran out of the house naked and bleeding" (Acts 19:13-17).

This is quite a story! Note that the men involved were not committed Christians but Jewish exorcists. Even those who were not Christians had seen the effect of the name of Jesus. Yet they mistakenly thought that by using a religious formula, inserting the magical words: *"In Jesus' name,"* they too would have authority. They did not realise that their own lives needed to be submitted to Jesus' authority. Because they were not under His authority they had neither His protection nor His power.

In contrast, consider another passage of scripture where the person involved *is* under Jesus' authority. *"Once, when we were going to the place of prayer, we were met by a slave girl who had a spirit by which she predicted the future. She earned a great deal of money for her owners by fortune-telling. This girl followed Paul and the rest of us, shouting, 'These men are servants of the Most High God, who are telling you the way to be saved.' She kept this up for many days. Finally Paul became so troubled that he turned round and said to the spirit, 'In the name of Jesus Christ I command you to come out of her.' At that moment the spirit left her"* (Acts 16:16-18). Because Paul was under Jesus' authority he was able to simply rebuke the spirit of divination in Jesus' name and she was free.

Like Paul, you and I are called to be effective fighters in the spiritual battle. Primarily this involves being submitted to Jesus' Lordship (see chapter seven), which means bringing every area of our lives under His authority and walking in humility.

As humility is the foundation of any authority given by the Lord, it's vital to maintain this attitude.

Remember that pride was at the root of the devil's fall. He exalted himself and was humbled as a result. We are therefore exhorted to *"submit yourselves, then, to God. Resist the devil and he will flee from you"* (James 4:7). Humility comes before spiritual authority can be exercised.

This truth hit home to me a few years ago when Kay and I were counselling a young man. Colin had recently given his life to the Lord but due to his past involvement with drugs was going through some struggles.

While praying together we had the impression that the devil had a doorway into Colin's mind, which was influencing his behaviour. As I'd been doing some study on the weapons of our warfare and felt fairly confident, I started to pray. I remember resisting the enemy in the name of Jesus and commanding him to go. I declared all the truths which came to mind and quoted the word of God. Yet all that happened was Colin started screaming – and he screamed and screamed and screamed!

I went through the whole procedure again and again, but Colin kept on screaming. I began to get a bit desperate, wondering if the neighbours would knock on the door at any moment to find out what was going on. Finally I came to the end of myself and said, "Lord, I don't know what to do. I can't do anything; it's over to You." And as soon as I said that, God met Colin. He quietened down immediately, sat up and his countenance was clear. The enemy's doorway was closed and instead Colin felt the Lord's peace filling his mind.

When I humbled myself, acknowledging that I couldn't do anything, God released His power into the situation. Nothing worked as long as I was putting my confidence in my understanding of the weapons and what I thought would work. Humility and authority go hand in hand.

Furthermore, if increasing authority is to be exercised to penetrate the devil's strongholds, Christian soldiers need to remember that in the spiritual battle they are not fighting each other; they're fighting against unseen powers! Remember Paul's statement that *"our struggle is not against flesh and blood, but against the rulers, against the authorities, against the powers of this dark world and against the spiritual forces of evil in the heavenly realms"* (Ephesians 6:12). Christians need to learn to identify the spiritual root of the problem confronting them, and then exercise authority to break the spiritual power, rather than expending energy fighting each other. Once again, this truth was highlighted for me in the following incident:–

I'd received a phone call from an elder of a church in which we'd previously had some involvement. Evidently the church was experiencing a clash over charismatic issues and things were going from bad to worse. In fact, at the previous elders' meeting they ended up shouting at each other and couldn't continue the meeting. That afternoon the elders were going to try and sort it all out, so my friend was asking us to pray.

In response, I telephoned a few others to join myself and Kay in prayer. Then, as we asked the Lord to show us what was really at the bottom of all this, several of us had the understanding that the enemy was seeking to cause division in the church and using the charismatic issue as the basis for attack.

So we began by submitting ourselves afresh to Jesus' Lordship; then declaring that Jesus was Lord over this church. We proclaimed His authority over the enemy and in Jesus' name, commanded the spirits of division and contention to flee. For quite some time we prayed in this manner, until there was a consensus among us that the spiritual forces of evil in the heavenly realms had been driven back.

Later that evening the elder rang me again. He was amazed at how different the meeting had been. Whereas before they had been attacking each other verbally, this time each had shared their point of view and some discussion followed, after which they all agreed to differ; they prayed and then went home. My friend's comment was significant: "It was as though all the fight had gone out of it!"

Peace and order came as we prayed. As we submitted ourselves to the authority of Jesus, and declared His authority in the situation, the battle was won. The spirits of division and contention had lost their power, and as a consequence, the church members stopped fighting each other on earth. (No doubt, others were also praying and contributing in this battle.)

Similarly, each one of us will be effective fighters in the spiritual battle as we learn to submit to Jesus' authority on a daily basis. It's not enough to speak words. Our lives must line up with what we're saying. As we align ourselves with His desires and plans, we will be able to pray effectively in His name, taking authority over the gates of hell.

Questions:

1. What does it mean to fight "in Jesus' name?"

2. What is the basis of our authority in the spiritual battle?

SECTION FOUR:
"LET'S FIGHT,
TOGETHER"

Chapter 17

Building Unity

So far we've considered the spiritual battle in terms of the individual soldier: you and me learning to stand and fight. However, most wars are not won by lone soldiers. Rather, victories take place because an army has successfully fought together.

When bombarded by an onslaught of arrows from the enemy, the Roman army would link their shields together, forming a solid wall against the enemy. Now was not the time to act as lone soldiers, engaging in hand to hand combat. It was the time to combine forces and move forward as an army.

Likewise, in the body of Christ, there are many times during the spiritual battle when it's necessary to fight as a united body of believers, rather than battling away as individuals. Unity, however, doesn't happen automatically. It requires work! A united spiritual army will only function effectively as Christians learn to link their lives together through open fellowship. This involves an honest sharing of our struggles and standing with one another in prayer.

The idea of being open and honest about our difficulties may sound foolish. If we believe this, the devil has achieved his goal. Remember, one of his master schemes is deception. He is aware of the strength of lives linked together under the lordship of Jesus, and wants to prevent that happening. His strategy is therefore to isolate Christians from the rest of the body by suggesting that no one else is experiencing difficulty; we are the only one. If this lie is believed, he knows that a willingness to share the struggle with others will be the last thing on our minds. As a result we struggle on as individual Christians, in defeat, on our own.

A number of people in a church or community may be under similar attack from the enemy at the same time, without realising it. They're experiencing common problems, but have been deceived into believing their difficulty is unique. This happened with Susan and Pauline.

Susan had worked for some time in a parish before coming to join one of our communities. In the past she'd taken on leadership functions with no problems but now found herself gripped by fear. Even the thought of making an announcement at a staff meeting caused her major stress. It was utterly ridiculous and yet she couldn't talk herself out of the anxiety or calm her fears in any way.

Pauline's fear was connected with singing. She'd sung in public on many occasions before coming to live in our community and was gifted in leading worship, yet the idea of doing so now was too overwhelming. On one occasion she'd tried to sing but found herself inhibited and unnaturally nervous. Since then she'd remained in the background, even though she knew the Lord was prompting her to be more involved.

Both girls felt very much alone in their fear, as though the problem must be them! It was not until a few general remarks were made over coffee one morning that they discovered they were each experiencing a similar struggle.

This realisation caused much relief for them both.

They discussed the matter further and began to recognise that the source of their problems lay in the devil's attack through fear. This discovery made them determined to fight the battle. As a result, Susan and Pauline began to pray together regularly, resisting the fear in the name of Jesus. In addition, they encouraged each other to take on new challenges. Over a period of time the gripping fear disappeared and their confidence was restored.

In both Susan and Pauline's lives, the initial key was for them to share their struggle with each other and pray together. Through being open and honest with each other they learnt to link their shields of faith together against the enemy. If we as the body of Christ are to be effective in repelling the devil's attacks and in fighting offensively, each one of us needs to be walking in open fellowship with other committed Christians.

How can Christians develop openness together? For a start, most people find it easier to relate honestly with a small group of people than to be vulnerable in a large group. Such a group can be as small as two or three people, preferably of the same sex. Jesus specifically mentioned that He'd meet with small groups of believers.[29]

If the group members are to experience spiritual growth together, commitment to the group will be necessary. Firstly, a commitment to make regular attendance at the meetings a priority. Secondly, a commitment to confidentiality. In other words, never to gossip about other people's problems. Those things discussed within the group are not matters for discussion with those outside the group. And thirdly, there needs to be a commitment to develop honesty with each other: in the good times and in the bad times.

It's the latter category which is often the hardest to put into practice. In the midst of a financial struggle, or a health problem, it can be difficult to be open about the situation with others. Yet many times victory in personal struggles will only be won when we allow the group to stand with us in prayer. This was certainly true for a fellow staff worker in recent months.

Caroline had looked depressed for quite a while, so when an opportunity arose I asked her if she was worried about something. Initially she was hesitant to respond, but after some moments she began to talk. During the past couple of weeks she'd been going through a financial crisis and hadn't been able to pay her bills for food and accommodation. As a result she'd become anxious and discouraged.

When Caroline first shared her need with me I felt that the devil had locked her into an attitude of unbelief. This was not only a battle in the physical realm, but also in the spiritual realm. We discussed this briefly and I tried to encourage her, but she wasn't very responsive.

A couple of weeks later, however, I met Caroline again and saw immediately that she looked different. She was much more positive. When I asked her what had happened, she told me that she'd shared her need with her church home group. They prayed together and within a week she'd received a financial gift from some friends who lived overseas. These friends were unaware of her need but felt prompted to send the money as a gift.

As I listened to Caroline's story and rejoiced with her I realised that openness with others had been an important key for her in fighting both the physical and the spiritual battle. (In saying this I don't mean that we should be open about our needs so that others will feel obliged to meet them; rather that as a body of believers we'll be committed to stand with each other and unite our faith to see the Lord provide.) For Caroline, openness with her home group was necessary so that she could break out of the spiritual bondage of unbelief. Once she'd shared her need with others they responded by praying together and their corporate faith encouraged her to trust afresh in the Lord's ability to provide. The Lord then prompted her other friends to meet her need for finance.

One of the results of honestly sharing weaknesses and strengths, and praying for each other, is that Christians become more effective as an army to fight offensively in the spiritual battle.

An example of the powerful results of openness and prayer is surely John Wesley's ministry many years ago in England. He established small group meetings throughout the country and took as his key verse, *"Confess your sins to each other and pray for each other so that you may be healed"* (James 5:16). These groups began putting this verse into practice as they met together.[30] And the result of their openness, humility and love for one another was not only that their lives were changed but, as they prayed with combined faith, the nation was changed and brought out of despair

As we commit ourselves to a lifestyle of openness as Christians, honest and relaxed relationships will be developed with one another. An increased level of trust and loyalty will be formed. And as we encourage each other, a greater release of life will be experienced in our church fellowships. The devil will not be able to work in such an environment. It will also enable us to corporately stand and see victory take place.

Therefore, *"let us consider how we may spur one another on towards love and good deeds. Let us not give up meeting together, as some are in the habit of doing, but let us encourage one another – and all the more as you see the Day approaching"* (Hebrews 10:24-5).

Questions:

1. Why are we more effective in the spiritual battle when we are in unity as Christians?

2. What are some of the results of openness amongst Christians?

3. What are the necessary ingredients for Biblical openness to develop?

Chapter 18

Fighting in Agreement

Christians will be an effective army in the spiritual battle as they learn to fight alongside each other – living their lives in open fellowship. Furthermore, effective corporate action will be taken against the unseen enemy as believers learn to agree together in prayer. Not in the passive verbal assent, "Yes, I agree with you," but agreement expressed in active participation with others in prayer.

When speaking to the early church Jesus said, "*I tell you that if two of you on earth agree about anything you ask for, it will be done for you by my Father in heaven. For where two or three come together in my name, there am I with them*" (Matthew 18:19-20).

The word "agree," as used in this verse, is translated from the Greek word "symphonio," a musical term meaning "harmony together." A group of musicians will only produce a harmonious sound as they ensure that their instruments are in tune and that they're all playing in the same key. Likewise, if "two or three" believers are to make a concerted attack against the unseen enemy in prayer, there needs to be a time of 'tuning in' to the Lord together, and then praying with joint understanding. As they take time to be still and listen to what He wants to say about a situation, He will then give direction and wisdom as a group how to pray effectively.

Within the context of a regular prayer group meeting a good way to actively 'tune in' to the Lord is to spend a few minutes in silence together. During this time each person should submit their own ideas to the Lord and then wait to hear Him speak to them in their heart. Note, it's important to realise that the Lord wants to speak to the whole group during this time, not just one or two individuals. As Jesus said to His disciples, *"when he, the Spirit of truth comes, he will guide you into all truth"* (John 16:13a). The "you" in this verse is plural, rather than singular. In other words, He's saying that "you" as the corporate body of Christ will be led into all truth. One person will not receive all truth. They will receive some and others will receive some.

Therefore, each member of the group should expect to receive from God part of the overall understanding needed to pray effectively. After a time of tuning in has passed, the leader of the group can then ask each person, "What do you think God is saying?" Someone may have an impression form in their mind about the nature of the devil's attack; another may recall a verse of Scripture; yet another may have a mental picture. As each individual contributes their thoughts, the Lord reveals corporate understanding to the group, together with His strategy on how to pray. Then they can begin to pray in agreement, concentrating on the subject of prayer, uniting their faith in the Lord to release His power into the situation.

During one group prayer several years ago I became aware of the powerful impact which praying in agreement together has upon the unseen world. We had been asked to pray for a young man who was in hospital with a recurring sickness. From the information we'd been given, we knew that the sickness was probably due to demonic oppression.

We waited in silence before the Lord as a group and after a time each person began to share their impressions, verses of Scripture and thoughts. Armed with the corporate understanding which God had given the group, we then began to pray for the young man, focusing our prayers together in agreement.

While one person prayed the others also verbalised their agreement. Then another person took up the same theme. In the midst of this the Lord gave Kay a picture in her mind of a door with the key in the lock. As the group continued to pray together, Kay saw that the key was turning, little by little, in the lock. The door was being unlocked as the group united in prayer together. When Kay described the picture she had we were all tremendously encouraged, realising the power of fighting in agreement.

Such agreement need not, however, be confined to formal prayer meetings. Jesus promised to be present where "two or three" are gathered together in His name. This can apply just as easily in a situation where two or three men are working together, when a friend comes around for coffee, or during a telephone conversation. At such times problems can often be discussed. It's only one step further to talk to the Lord about it and ask for His wisdom together. It is the one step the devil does not want us to take, as he knows only too well the powerful effect of twos and threes agreeing together in prayer.

One common grouping of "twos" is, of course, the married couple. Yet many couples find it difficult to pray together. (Has it ever occured to you that the devil might have a hand in this at all?)

When Kay and I got married we needed to learn how to pray together, rather than as two separate individuals. In our early attempts at praying together we tended to end up frustrated, and after a while it was obvious that we needed to talk things through.

As I'm somewhat of an extrovert in the way I pray, I feel comfortable adlibbing my prayers, and can do so for quite a time. Kay, on the other hand, has a more introverted personality and had more difficulty in praying out loud. Discussing these differences helped us to understand one another better, to realise where we each needed to make room for the other person.

This meant that I had to learn to express one thought, keeping my prayer fairly short and to the point, so that Kay could pick it up and add her voice. Equally, Kay needed to listen to what I was saying so she could agree with my prayer and verbalise her own thoughts, rather than thinking about what she was going to pray next.

We also realised that the "holy aura" often associated with prayer was not necessary. In fact, instead of making little speeches to God, we recognised that it was okay to stop and talk – to discuss what we'd been praying – and then to pray some more.

Learning to make room for one another, allowing for interruption and discussion, is all part of the flow of harmonious prayer. The result is agreement, and where two or three agree, *"it shall be done,"* for *"there I am with them,"* Jesus said.

I believe that one of the reasons the devil does all he can to prevent married couples praying together is that he recognises the power of agreement. Through prayer together married couples can affect the spiritual realm, particularly with regard to their families. This is just what the devil does not want to see happen, as he has declared war on family life

– perhaps more evident in this generation than at any other time in history.

Part of God's answer to the enemy's schemes is for married couples to exercise spiritual authority at home and fight in agreement against the enemy. We should not accept the influence of the enemy in our children's lives, but we should learn to recognise his activity and rise up together and take action.

As parents, Kay and I needed to take our authority in the spiritual realm not long after we moved into our present home. Our daughter had developed a friendship with a girl at school. As they spent more time together, however, we noticed a change in her attitude. She started to speak negatively about herself and became careless in her jobs around the home, attitudes which were unusual.

Kay and I were praying separately about the visible changes we were observing on our daughter, and had done so for some weeks. Yet it was only when we together asked the Lord for His help that He showed us the invisible source of the problem. Her friend was communicating a wrong spirit in their relationship, which was having a negative effect upon her behaviour.

As we prayed together we sensed that we should *not* speak to our daughter but we should resist the enemy in the name of Jesus. So we took authority over the wrong spirit which was influencing her life, in the name of Jesus, and asked God to do His work in the situation.

The very next morning our daughter casually mentioned to us that the Lord had shown her she was spending too much time with this one friend at school and allowing herself to be influenced in a negative way. We were amazed at how quickly the Lord worked when we agreed in prayer together.

Over the next few weeks whenever our daughter was with her friend, in her heart she resisted the wrong spiritual influence, and as time passed her circle of friends widened, so that she wasn't spending all her time with this one girl.

Kay and I saw a positive change take place in our daughter *after* we'd prayed together. It was as we sought the Lord together that we received mutual understanding of the enemy's influence and were able to agree together to bind and break his power.

Whether agreement in prayer takes place between married couples or single people involved in prayer partnerships, whether it be spontaneously offered or within the context of a planned meeting, its impact upon the unseen realm is powerful. As God's people learn what it is to tune into the Lord and then pray accordingly, spiritual battles will be won. Let us therefore determine in our hearts to take advantage of situations (spontaneous or planned) where, as two or three "gathered together," we can fight in agreement against the enemy.

Questions:

1. What does it mean for two or three to agree together?

2. How can we learn to pray together more effectively?

Chapter 19

Fighting For Others

Fighting alongside each other in the spiritual battle involves uniting forces to see the devil's influence broken in our lives as Christians. It also means waging war against his influence in the lives of non-Christians: in particular, family or close friends who are not committed to the Lord.

In many cases people who are close to us can seem to be the hardest to reach for the Lord. Attempts to share one's faith with family members often ends in apparent failure. This can be partly due to parents and brothers and sisters knowing us too well to be impressed by our words. Or perhaps in the attempt to testify about God's love, the discussion has got heated and ended up in argument, which has the effect of negating what's been said.

The devil will readily remind Christians of such times, suggesting that they've "failed" or that it's pointless to talk again; a waste of time even to pray! His goal is to discourage us so that we give up!

Yet as Paul reminds the church, *"our struggle is not against flesh and blood* (therefore it won't be won through persuasive speech, defensiveness, arguments etc), *but against the rulers, against the authorities, against the powers of this dark world and against the spiritual forces of evil in the heavenly realms"* (Ephesians 6:12). Spiritual weapons need to be employed. And as discussed in the previous chapter, Jesus promises to give His people spiritual keys to unlock doors, both in the heavenly realm and on earth. These keys are not limited in power. They can be used with authority on behalf of all people, including unsaved family and friends.

Some Christians tend to back away from this idea, assuming that if they start talking about the devil working in people, it suggests that they're demon possessed. Although that is not normally the case, unsaved people are under an influence. The Bible says that if we're not under the authority of Jesus we're under the authority of the enemy.[31] We, who have been brought into the kingdom of light, can overcome the enemy on behalf of others as we fight for them together in the name of Jesus. The following story is a good example:–

Richard was a good friend of mine. We'd known each other for some eight or nine years and throughout that time I'd been impressed by his commitment to prayer. He prayed regularly for his friends and relatives who did not know the Lord and was particularly concerned for his father, a man called John. Richard and I often prayed together, focusing many times on John's need for salvation. There appeared to be very little change taking place until Richard discovered a booklet about prayer for the unsaved.

Written by a missionary, this little book tells the story of her prayer battle for the unsaved members of her family. She had prayed for each one of them for many years without seeing any change. However, when she began to take authority in prayer over the powers of darkness, as led by the Holy Spirit, changes began to happen.

This lady's testimony was such an encouragement to Richard that we began following her example. Firstly, we began to ask the Lord for specific scriptures to use when praying for John. One which the Lord brought to our attention was, *"We demolish arguments and every pretension that sets itself up against the knowledge of God, and we take captive every thought to make it obedient to Christ"* (2 Corinthians 10:5). So we started to declare the truth of that verse on behalf of John.

Continuing to use this scripture, we asked the Lord, "What are the particular strongholds in John's mind?" "Prejudice" was one of the areas impressed upon our minds. In thinking it over, Richard could see that this was true. His father was especially prejudiced against the church. Richard just had to mention something about God or Jesus and his father would say, "Oh, you mean the church. All they're after is your money," and he'd refuse to discuss anything spiritual in a reasonable way.

Recognising the reality of this prejudice, Richard and I prayed accordingly. John's prejudice was giving the devil the right to oppress him. However, we agreed with God that Jesus died on the Cross to redeem John from his old way of life and to cleanse him from sin – including prejudice. So we prayed, "Lord Jesus, thank you that you bore John's sin on the Cross and broke the power of the devil's influence. Therefore, in your name we pull down the stronghold of prejudice in his life." We then asked the Holy Spirit to bring His influence into John's mind, bringing thoughts of truth, so John would have a new ability to see other people's points of view.

As Richard and I continued to ask the Lord how to pray for John we became aware of another stronghold which needed to be broken, the stronghold of unbelief. This realisation came when Richard looked up a scripture reference the Holy Spirit

129

impressed upon his mind. He read the words, *"the god of this age has blinded the minds of unbelievers, so that they cannot see the light of the gospel of the glory of Christ, who is the image of God"* (2 Corinthians 4:4).

Richard began to see that his father's resistance to the Gospel was not based solely on his own refusal to believe, but was also reinforced by the devil's blinding influence.

Armed with this understanding we prayed, resisting the devil's blindness over John's mind in the name of Jesus. Declaring the truth that Jesus came into the world to destroy the works of the devil,[32] and that on the Cross He rendered the devil powerless,[33] we stood against the spirit of unbelief over John's life. This way we used the *"sword of the Spirit,"* wielded the *"shield of faith"* and put on the *"helmet of salvation,"* asking the Lord to shine His light of truth into John's mind and heart so that he would believe the truth about the Gospel.

We persevered in prayer for John over several months. As John lived several hundred miles away, Richard didn't have any visible indication of change taking place. It was a case of putting his confidence in God's character and choosing to believe the truth of His Word.

However, four months later, Richard's family gathered together for a long weekend. As they sat down to the evening meal, his father hesitantly asked, "Um . . ., Richard, would you say grace please?" Recalling this, Richard said, "I was totally amazed, as we'd never prayed in our home at the meal table."

Returning home after the weekend Richard and I prayed with increasing vigour for John. This time the impression at the forefront of Richard's mind was that "the price has been paid" and he began to realise afresh that Jesus had shed His blood for his father. Whatever the prejudices, or unbelief in his mind, the blood of Jesus paid the price for his father's salvation.

Richard told me, "I realise that it's not that we've found the right technique of praying for my father; nor am I trying to negate the effect of other's prayers. It's as though the Lord is giving me new revelation of what He's done on the Cross and showing me that although the devil has been influencing my father's mind for so long, his power is not as great as the power of God. I've needed to see that."

Throughout the following months as we prayed, exercising authority over the powers of darkness, John's attitude towards the Lord gradually changed. The tone of his letters to his son was different; a softening seemed to be taking place. What we didn't know was that during this time, one of John's friends was prompted by the Lord to send him a book. Yet another invited him to attend a concert where a well known Christian musician not only performed but also gave his testimony of how Jesus had become real to him. Both these occasions made quite an impact on him.

Eight months after we began praying for John, Richard was talking with a friend on the phone. "Isn't it great what happened to your father last week?" his friend exclaimed. "What was that?" Richard asked. "Didn't you know?" was the reply. "He gave his life to the Lord."

A few days later Richard received a letter from his father. It was written in completely unevangelical language and simply told him that one morning "all my doubts were gone," and in their place "I realised my need for God".

After his father had reached this conclusion he had

gone to see a friend of his, a Christian. As they talked together it was obvious that John was under conviction and it was relatively easy for the friend to explain salvation to him and lead him to the Lord.

As Richard told me about the contents of John's letter, he exclaimed, "My father is a changed man!" We rejoiced together!

This event made quite an impact upon me, for it was clear that major changes occured in Richard's father when the prayer emphasis became spiritual warfare. When we took offensive action against the enemy, using our authority as sons of God to proclaim the power of the blood of Jesus over John's life the hold that the enemy had over his life was broken.

As a result of this experience, and others since, I firmly believe that we need to be much more active in recognizing the works of the enemy in unsaved people and more active in waging war, on their behalf, in the spiritual realm. Today, as perhaps never before, the challenge before us as God's people is to fight on the offensive against the unseen enemy, who will be trying to influence our families. Yet instead of allowing that awareness to foster discouragement or hopelessness, let us engage in the battle, taking authority over the powers of darkness as the Lord leads us.

Questions:

1. Why is it important to exercise spiritual weapons when we pray for unsaved people, rather than general prayers for their salvation?

2. Are there people in your family who are not committed Christians? If so, ask the Lord for His strategy on how to pray for them.

Chapter 20

Fighting For Change

Central to this discussion on spiritual warfare is the power of Jesus' death on the Cross and the triumph of His resurrection. *"The reason the Son of God appeared was to destroy the devil's work"* (1 John 3:8). And on the Cross Jesus did just that. He *"rendered the devil powerless"* so that we might be reconciled to God.

Yet it was not just for you and I as individuals. Redemption extends to every area of society which has been corrupted through selfish men and women, influenced by the devil. For example, the areas of education, business, government, media and so on, have all been reconciled to God through the Cross.[34]

For many Christians this is a totally neglected application of the Cross of Jesus. It's one thing to believe in personal salvation; it seems more difficult to believe that the thinking of society can be changed. And that's exactly what the devil wants people to think!

Christians have listened to the devil's lies about their own lives and they've listened to his lies concerning the state of society; lies which cause them to view the world through the eyes of doom. By believing that society is unredeemable, we've limited the power of the Cross and resurrection.

Yet when Jesus appeared to His disciples after the

resurrection He said, *"All authority in heaven and on earth has been given to me. Therefore go and make disciples of all nations. . ."* (Matthew 28:18-19). How is a nation discipled? By God's people, the church – Christians influencing society to think and live according to Biblical values.

If we stop to consider society today we find that many of its activities are based on thinking contrary to Biblical values. Education was originally founded on Biblical principles yet today's schools are now based on secular humanism, that is human reasoning which excludes God. Think also about the increasing violence in our towns and cities, much of which can be attributed to the influence of violent films on television and video upon impressionable minds. As the Bible says, the whole world is under the influence of the evil one.[35] Yet as we've also read, *"the reason the Son of God appeared was to destroy the devil's work."* Jesus reconciled *all* areas of society to Himself on the Cross and He commissions us as His church to see them redeemed here on earth. Obviously there is a limit to what we can achieve before Jesus returns to fully establish His kingdom. Nevertheless, He calls us to fight for change in the thinking and activities of the societies in which we live. How do we fight for change?

We need to challenge the spiritual powers which are binding the world's thinking and blocking its submission to the lordship of Jesus. This will be partly achieved as Christians get involved in places of influence within society. But the spiritual powers also need to be dismantled through prayer. As believers gather together, submitted to the lordship of Jesus and in agreement with Him and each other, He will give them keys to unlock the devil's hold. Let me give you an example.

A friend of mine who lives in New Zealand recently told me about a situation which took place near his home town. In this town, the drug scene, feminism, New Age and so forth, dominate the local school. While education in New Zealand is secular, schools do have the opportunity to have weekly religious instruction, called "Bible in Schools." However, the school committee in Andrew's town had resisted this opportunity.

Two years ago some of the parents, who are members of Andrew's church, decided they wanted to do something to change the situation. Firstly, they began to pray together. Then they approached the school committee, asking them to reconsider and include " Bible in Schools" in the curriculum. The committee refused.

The group then canvassed the parents of children who attended the school and discovered that the majority were not against "Bible in Schools". Heartened by this realisation they held a public meeting. As a result, they eventually persuaded the school committee to have a referendum on the issue.

The results of the referendum were 52 families for "Bible in Schools" and 48 families against. It looked as though they had the victory. However, the school committee then decided to count the number of children in the families, rather than count the number of families. That way the score was 49 children for "Bible in Schools" and 51 children against. It was a battle!

Yet the concerned parents did not give up. Shortly afterwards, elections were announced for a new board of school trustees. They went to the Lord in prayer and as a result, they decided that some amongst them should offer themselves as candidates. Concluding his story Andrew said, "Out of the five candidates who were elected, four of them were Christian parents. Subsequently, "Bible in Schools" was included in the curriculum!"

What interested me was that these people not only prayed but also acted. (Remember the Biblical story we considered in chapter two, where Moses exercised spiritual authority and Joshua exercised physical authority. Work in both levels brought victory to God's people.) They'd taken on a project, done their homework, prayed and exercised spiritual warfare – and having been involved in both these dimensions they'd influenced their society. It was a small beginning but it was a beginning!

In a similar vein, Andrew recounted another story which illustrated how Christians can effectively be involved in the spiritual fight and see changes take place in their society.

In Andrew's local town, about five years ago, there was a gang known as the "Mongrel Mob." Part of a nation-wide gang, the youths were a wild bunch who sometimes engaged in occultic activities and were often in trouble with the police.

Andrew recalled that the police declared an amnesty if people handed in their unregistered fire arms. Following this announcement a request came from the local Mongrel Mob to use his church as an intermediary place between the gang and the police. The church elders agreed and at the resulting meeting gang members brought their sawn-off shotguns, wrapped in newspaper, and gave them to the police.

Once the meeting was over the gang members were sitting around, bemoaning the fact that they were continually in and out of jail, and often had nowhere to sleep, except in the back of cars. It was a real cry for help.

Andrew's church ran an employment training project in horticulture and thinking that the gang members would be better off growing cabbages than burgling people's homes, the elders of the church approached the labour department to see if this could be arranged. The department agreed to a six month trial period.

The six months stretched to five years and it was a time of learning for everyone concerned. It certainly wasn't easy! Yet as well as getting involved with the gang, the church members also prayed.

Andrew recalled, "One of the first things which happened was the Lord spoke to us clearly that the boys were *not* Mongrels; nor were they a mob! Rather they were young people whom He loved, who needed to change their ways. As we began to view them in this light our fear and anxiety about them was eliminated."

As the prayer meetings continued the church members prayed against the spiritual forces of evil which were influencing the gang members. Their awareness of the spiritual battle was heightened following an incident when a couple of young people decided to leave the gang. Although they were smuggled away from the gang and out of harm's way, they were subsequently discovered and badly beaten up. This often happens when people try to leave a group which is influenced by the occult. It was not enough for the members to decide to leave the gang; there were also oppressive spiritual forces from which they needed to be set free.

However, the Christians began to see positive results in the battle. On the night when the Mongrel Mob were to hold a big gathering of local groups, a further prayer meeting was held at which the church members were agreeing in prayer and standing against the enemy. The building where the gang's meeting was scheduled to take place suddenly caught fire and the whole place was burnt to ashes, including all the occult symbols they'd put up on the walls. (The arsonist was never found, but the church did not rule out fire from heaven!)

Nine months later, the local gang members decided they were no longer going to associate with the Mongrel Mob, and they closed their operations down. In Andrew's town at least, the Mongrel Mob ceased to exist and out of the fourteen youths who began the employment training scheme only one is currently out of work.

In concluding his story, Andrew commented that if the church members had just got involved with the gang in training them for work skills they would still be in training. Prayer had to be involved. Similarly, if the church had just prayed and had not got physically involved with the young people, they would not have seen change occur. The battle was only fought successfully when the church became involved in both dimensions.

These examples, though hard battles, are small beginnings. Yet that is how we can get started in the spiritual fight for change. Rather than read and watch events taking place around us with a sense of defeat, we can group together and learn how to fight for change. Nothing is impossible!

I believe God is calling us today to redeem our families, systems of government, medicine, media, business and education – every area of life. Obviously this will take much perseverance. There are many challenges before us. One current challenge is the increasing influence of false religions in our nations. Such a challenge will only be surmounted as the whole body of Christ is involved in praying and doing spiritual battle, actively standing against the enemy, and also preaching the Gospel and sharing the love of Jesus with the people.

You and I have received a battle charge: to stand up and fight, that together we might plunder the gates of hell! Jesus said, *"the gates of Hades shall not hold out against the church"* (Matthew 16:18 Amplified Bible). As members of the body of Christ we're not meant to be passive in the spiritual battle. Quite the opposite.[36] We are called to be actively involved in the battle, working in partnership with Jesus to see His kingdom established here on earth. Let us take hold of our calling, personally in our daily lives and corporately as a church, to plunder the strongholds of Satan where people and societies are held captive. Let us stand up and fight!

Questions:

1. In what areas did Jesus render the devil powerless on the Cross?

2. Which issues in your education system, government, media etc., are you concerned about?

3. How do you think you can take action and fight for change?

Notes

(1)   Colossians 1:13

(2)   1 Peter 5:8

(3)   Psalm 62:8

(4)   James 4:7

(5)   See also Psalm 147:5

(6)   See Isaiah 40:13-14

(7)   Genesis 1:26-27

(8)   A.H. Strong, "Systematic Theology" p. 271

(9)   Leviticus 16:34

(10) 1 Peter 2:24

(11) 2 Corinthians 5:21

(12) Matthew 27:46

(13) Acts 2:24

(14) Hebrews 2:14-15

(15) Matthew 24:28

(16) Acts 26:2-11

(17) Luke 3:22; 4:1

(18) Acts 2:4

(19) A. Skevington Wood, "The Expositors Bible Commentary Volume 2," Frank E. Gaebelein Gen. Ed. Zondervan 1978

(20) Ephesians 5:18

(21) John 1:12

(22) 1 John 3:1

(23) Isaiah 53:3

(24) 1 Peter 2:24

(25) 2 Samuel 11:14-21

(26) 2 Corinthians 10:5b

(27) Psalm 19:1

(28) Philippians 2:12

(29) Matthew 18:18-19

(30) "The Radical Wesley and Patterns for Church Renewal" by Howard A. Snyder, I.V.P. 1980

(31) Colossians 1:13-14 Ephesians 2:1-3

(32) 1 John 3:8

(33) Hebrews 2:14

(34) Colossians 1:19-20

(35) 1 John 5:19

(36) Jude verse 23

Appendix 1:

Victory Over the Occult

"Submit yourselves, then, to God. Resist the devil and he will flee from you" (James 4:7).

As you have been reading this book it may be that some of the references to the occult, or some of the examples given, have reminded you of times in your life when you've dabbled in these areas. If this is so, I encourage you to read this section through carefully and to follow through with the application given.

At the present time we are witnessing a rapid growth of occult religions and practices. Many people, including Christians, have been involved in the occult without being aware how strongly the Bible condemns such practices. Experience has shown that involvement in these things can bring damage to the mind and spirit of an individual and even minor contact can seriously damage spiritual growth.

In the Old Testament scripture is very clear about avoiding all occult practices: *"Let no-one be found among you who sacrifices his son or daughter in the fire, who practices divination or sorcery, interprets omens, engages in witchcraft, or casts spells, or who is a medium, or spiritist or who consults the dead. Anyone who does these things is detestable to the Lord."* (Deuteronomy 18:10:-12).

143

Present day versions of these things include fortune telling, ouija boards, seances of various kinds, black or white magic, palm reading, divining rods or pendulums etc. Any practice which attempts to obtain supernatural power or knowledge (even if for apparently good reasons like healing the body or knowing the future) which does not operate through the direct agency of our Lord Jesus Christ is not of God.

Other dangerous practices are hypnotism (yielding the mind and personality to a person other than God, who alone has the right), secret societies and lodges (requiring Christians to enter into vows and covenants with unbelievers), eastern religions and their western counterparts (yoga, transcendental meditation, the martial arts, etc).

Our God is a supernatural God who enables His servants to perform miracles of power and have revelation and utterance, through the gifts of the Spirit, as outlined in chapters twelve and fourteen of the first letter to the Corinthians. He does this as a demonstration of His love and to bring liberty to His people. But Satan tries to deceive people by his counterfeit methods, so that he can bring them under his control.

How, then, can we be free? Firstly, we need to focus on Jesus, our deliverer.

"The reason the Son of God appeared was to destroy the devil's work" (1 John 3:8).

"And having disarmed the powers and authorities, he made a public spectacle of them, triumphing over them by the Cross" (Colossians 2:15).

"Since the children have flesh and blood, he too shared in their humanity so that by his death he might destroy him who holds the power of death – that is, the devil – and free those who all their lives were held in slavery by their fear of death" (Hebrews 2:14-15).

Steps to Deliverance

1. Confess your sin

Each contact with powers of darkness must be confessed individually to the Lord as sin. It is through confession that we can then appropriate the cleansing blood of Christ.

"If we confess our sins, He is faithful and just and will forgive us our sins and purify us from all unrighteousness " (1 John 1:7,9).

2. Declare Jesus to be Lord of Your Life

This means to openly acknowledge that you are submitting control of your life to the Lord Jesus Christ, especially any area in which you've sought help from the powers of darkness (e.g. your health, concern for the future etc.).

". . . if you confess with your mouth, 'Jesus is Lord,' and believe in your heart that God raised Him from the dead, you will be saved" (Romans 10:9).

3. Renounce the Works of the Devil

This is a verbal declaration that you are giving up and casting off all association or contact with the powers of darkness, never to be involved again, *". . . that they may turn from darkness to light and from the power of Satan to God, that they may receive forgiveness of sins"* (Acts 26:18 RSV).

To turn from darkness also means that all objects such as books, charms and artifacts associated with the occult must be destroyed.

"Many of those who believed now came and openly confessed their evil deeds. A number who practiced sorcery brought their scrolls together and burned them publicly. When they calculated the value of the scrolls, the total came to fifty thousand drachmas. In this way the word of the Lord spread widely and grew in power" (Acts 19:18-20).

4. Pray With Someone Who Knows Their Authority Over the Enemy

This step may not always be necessary but it will be, if involvement in the occult has been extensive. Very often involvement has brought other problems, such as fear and unbelief, which make it difficult for the person to deal with the devil on his own. Praying with a mature Christian, who knows how to resist the devil and break his power, will bring the deliverance.

"Therefore confess your sins to each other and pray for each other so that you may be healed" (James 5:16).

"He has delivered us from the dominion of darkness and transferred us to the kingdom of his beloved Son, in whom we have redemption, the forgiveness of sins" (Colossians 1:13 RSV).

If you have followed the above steps you have been **separated** from the powers of darkness. Stand firm on this promise!

Appendix 2:

Suggestions for Encouraging Openness in Home Groups

When meeting together with a small group of Christians it's useful to have some means of stimulating openness. (Please remember if you're leading a group that although people should be encouraged to be open with one another it should never be forced. A loving atmosphere of caring for each other will never be achieved with heavy handed leaders forcing people to share things when they're not ready for it.) At times it can be helpful to ask a few questions, such as the following:

1. How is your relationship with the Lord?

2. Are you finding prayer to be effective and fulfilling?

3. Are you finding Bible readings to be stimulating?

4. Are you having any problems in your relationships with other people?

5. Are you being fulfilled in your daily work?

6. Is your financial situation satisfactory?

7. Are you having problems with negative thoughts?

8. Are you sharing your faith with unbelievers?

These questions obviously cover foundational areas: areas of growth in which all Christians need to be encouraged regularly. You may wish to adapt them to suit your particular situation. They are intended only as a guideline.

If you have enjoyed this book and would like to help us to send a copy of it and many other titles to needy pastors in the **Third World**, please write for further information or send your gift to:

Sovereign World Trust
PO Box 777, Tonbridge
Kent TN11 9XT
United Kingdom

or to the **'Sovereign World'** distributor
in your country.

If sending money from outside the United Kingdom, please send an International Money Order or Foreign Bank Draft in STERLING, drawn on a **UK** bank to **Sovereign World Trust**.